How to Be Debt-Free
(Formerly published as "Your Road to Wealth Starts Here")

by Avery Breyer

Copyright © 2016 Avery Breyer Inc. All rights reserved worldwide.

A note from the author: *Personally, I'd rather leave things to common sense, good ethics, and everyone having a sense of personal responsibility for their actions. And like any decent person should do, obviously I do my best to provide accurate information at all times. But the experts say it's better to put proper disclaimers in place, so here goes...*

ALL RIGHTS RESERVED. No part of this material may be used, reproduced, distributed or transmitted in any form and by any means whatsoever, including without limitation photocopying, recording or other electronic or mechanical methods or by any information storage and retrieval system, without the prior written permission from the author, except for brief excepts in a review.

DISCLAIMER. This, and other books by Avery Breyer are intended to provide only general information on personal finance, credit scores, building wealth, real estate, lifestyle design, work from home opportunities, and other topics. No investment, tax, legal, or insurance advice is intended or given. Investment decisions are subject to certain risk factors that may not be discussed completely, or at all, in this book. Your Investment decisions and strategies should be determined solely by you in the exercise of your own judgment based on your unique investment objectives and financial circumstances. If you need professional advice, you should consult your own professional advisers. Neither the author, Avery Breyer Inc. nor publisher provide any legal or other professional advice. If you need professional advice, you should seek advice from the appropriate licensed professional. This book does not provide complete information on the subject matter covered. This book is not intended to address specific requirements, either for an individual or an organization. This book is intended to be used only as a general guide, and not as a sole source of information on the subject matter. While the author has undertaken diligent efforts to ensure accuracy, there is no guarantee of accuracy or of no errors, omissions or typographical errors. Any slights of people or organizations are unintentional. Any reference to any person or organization whether living or dead is purely coincidental. The author and publisher shall have no liability or responsibility to any person or entity and hereby disclaim all liability, including without limitation, liability for consequential damages regarding any claim, loss or damage that may be incurred, or alleged to have been incurred, directly or indirectly, arising out of the information provided in this book.

The information presented herein represents the view of the author as of the date of publication. Because of the rate with which conditions change, the author reserves the right to alter and/or update her opinion based on the new conditions, and the author is not obligated to update this information.

Anything written in this book that contains the views of others has either been submitted to the author (or Avery Breyer Inc.), or found on the Internet and published as a fair use. Any views expressed in this book by 3rd party authors or contributors are solely those of 3rd party authors or contributors and do not in any way reflect the views of the author or Avery Breyer Inc. This book is solely a provider of useful information and hereby disclaims all liability for any damages or injury or other harm arising from this book. The author and Avery Breyer Inc. are not obligated to update any information attributable to 3rd party authors or contributors.

READ THIS FIRST!

As thanks for buying my book, I'd like to offer you **FREE access to 3 special bonuses I've prepared especially for you, that will help you on your journey.**

Here's what you get:

1. Instant access to my **Debt Destroyer Tool**
2. One day after that, you'll get access to my very informative **video interview with debt destroying dynamo Melanie Lockert.** This interview is **jam-packed with actionable tips** on handling the emotional highs and lows of dealing with debt, tips **for the average person** on how to get rid of it quicker, and so much more.
3. And a few days after that, you'll get access to an info-packed **interview with personal finance expert Michelle Schroeder-Gardner** — she has 2 undergrad degrees plus a **Finance MBA**, and **paid off her debts in only 7 months.** Listen to her interview and learn how to pull it off. She really knows her stuff!

Last, but not least, if I ever come across any other info that I think will be of use to you, I'll be sure to send it your way.

<u>You're not alone in your journey to destroy your debt and feel the freedom that comes with that. Others have walked this path before you and are here to help.</u> Ready?

Get Access Now!
https://averybreyer.com/your-road-to-wealth-starts-here-1/

Contents

Introduction…..7

The 7 Big Lies You've Been Told About Debt…..11

Good Debt Versus Bad Debt…..30

Mortgages…..43

The Power Pay Off Plan (and How Sam Saved 20 Grand)…..53

The Secrets to Successfully Get Rid of Debt…..64

Where to Find the Money…..73

How Much Should You Pay Towards Your Debts…..81

The Truth About Debt Consolidation…..87

Insurance For the Unexpected…..91

Action Steps Recap…..97

Building Wealth…..99

More Books by Avery Breyer…..102

Appendix…..105

Introduction

"A man in debt is so far a slave." Ralph Waldo Emerson

Do you owe too much money? Are your debts crushing your spirit, embarrassing you, and stressing you out?

You're not alone. The good news is that you can fix that. And this book will show you how.

Imagine this scenario.

You're no longer a slave to bad debt. Student loans, your mortgage, car loans, and credit card debt are all in the past. Creditors aren't bothering you.

You finally have enough cash to pay for necessities every month, and can afford some fun stuff too. You can give money to causes that are important to you, and help out your loved ones when they need you. Your net worth is growing, and your sense of financial security gets better every day. You simply don't have to worry about money anymore.

Well guess what?

All of that can be your reality. You have the power to make that happen.

And here's the thing. It isn't as hard to accomplish as you may think.

It begins here, with one simple thing that will completely transform your finances, now and forever. You get rid of your debts, transform your finances, and use the money that's been freed up to build your wealth.

You're about to see simple ways to get rid of the bad debts that are ruining your cash flow. And, you'll find out…

- The seven big lies you've been told
- How to tell the difference between good and bad debt
- Whether your mortgage is good or bad (the answer may surprise you!)
- The Power Pay Off Plan to become debt-free (and how Sam saved 20 grand)
- The secrets to successfully get rid of debt
- Where to find the money to do all this
- How much you ought to be paying towards your debts
- The truth about debt consolidation (including pitfalls to avoid)
- How to use insurance to protect yourself from the unexpected
- What to do next

You're about to learn time-tested strategies for winning your battles with debt.

And I'm also going to share with you some strategies for increasing your income, as well as some important precautions you can take to minimize the risk of unforeseen events ruining your plans.

My background

I have no credit card debt (I pay them off in full each month), and no student loans either. I paid off my first (and only) $20,000+ car loan way ahead of schedule. And for good measure, we paid off the mortgage for our first home in less than five years. My credit score is excellent, a little under 800 (last I checked).

And I'm going to show you how to do it too.

Who this book is for…

If you're looking for a clear roadmap with a step-by-step plan that's simple for the average person to follow and implement, you're in the right place.

You don't have to be rich to do this. All you need is to be willing to do the work, and be patient enough to wait for the right opportunities.

And be ready to roll up your sleeves and get rid of debt with integrity and honesty. No shady tricks.

What this book is NOT…

This book is not about how to file for bankruptcy. Nor is it about creating a new identity to fool creditors into thinking you've disappeared off the face of the planet.

If you're looking for a "revolutionary" plan to get rid of debt with little to no effort — *a magic elixir of sorts* — you're in the wrong place.

And anyone who tells you that they have a "new", "novel", or otherwise special way to get rid of debt is full of crap. Sorry for being so blunt, but it needed to be said.

My promise to you…

I promise that your road to better finances can start here if you have focus, determination and are willing to put in the work.

On the other hand, if you're looking for a magic bullet (which doesn't exist, by the way, and I'll discuss some of them in this book), you'll be distracted and less likely to pull this off.

And don't confuse complexity with superiority. There's no need to over-complicate this.

What you're about to read in this book is simple, down-to-earth, time-tested advice that can work for anyone. This book will show you how to get rid of your debt with your head held high when the topic of money comes up with people you know.

The longer you wait, the worse it gets — so let me show you how to destroy your debts, starting now.

"Chains of habit are too light to be felt until they are too heavy to be broken." Warren Buffett

Take action now, before it's too late.

Your debts are a leech on your bank account. If you do nothing, a steady stream of your hard-earned cash will continue making your lenders rich, instead of you. These payments will steal your ability to pay for things that are important to you. You work hard for your money, and deserve to keep more of it.

It's time to put an end to being an average person struggling with debt, and feel confident about your finances instead.

Are you ready? Let's do this.

The first step is to keep reading.

The 7 Big Lies You've Been Told About Debt

"A lie can travel half way around the world while the truth is still putting on its shoes." Charles Spurgeon

Succumbing to lies and misleading information is a dangerous thing when it comes to debt, and can cost you a lot of money if you're not careful. Don't let that happen to you.

You're about to learn seven big lies you've been told about debt, and be protected against them forever.

Part of the problem is that good lies often run rampant because most of us are too busy to go out and research every single claim we see.

"A lie told often enough becomes the truth." Vladimir Lenin

On top of it all, research shows that if we're told a lie repeatedly, we are more likely to accept it as truth.

There was an interesting study done on this in 2015, published in the Journal of Experimental Psychology[1]. They found that the more often we hear a false statement, the easier it is for us to process that information. And the easier it is for us to process the information, the more likely we are to believe it.

The shocking thing is that this even applies to false information that we already know to be false.

I know, that sounds crazy, right?

Apparently, when we are deciding whether or not a piece of information is accurate, we sometimes forget to consider what we already know, and instead take a shortcut by allowing the frequent repetition of a statement to convince us that it simply must be true.

So knowing that, reading this chapter could be dangerous.

Because if all you do is skim it over, focusing on the sub-headlines, without really taking the time to immerse yourself in the reasons why these lies are untrue, you may end up making yourself more likely to believe them in future. If it's easier for your brain to process the quick and easy soundbite — the lies in the sub-headlines — you may end up believing them.

So don't do that, okay? And maybe you ought to protect yourself against some of these untruths by reading this chapter several times over so the rebuttals to the lies are firmly entrenched in your mind.

Alright, now it's time to debunk some of the most common misinformation that you've been told.

LIE! Getting a 30-year mortgage for your home is the right thing to do

I recommend that you do everything in your power to avoid signing yourself up for a 30-year mortgage for your home.

Most people believe that a lifetime of mortgage payments is normal, and pretty much a requirement if one wants to own a home. Banks and credit unions do little or nothing to correct this assumption, happily signing purchasers up for a 30-year mortgage, knowing that they'll make a killing over that time frame via the interest being charged.

Say Amanda and Michael buy a $300,000 home, and put a 20% down payment on it.

Let's also say that they get a 30-year mortgage with interest rates locked in at only 3.75%. By the end of 30 years, they'll have paid the bank just over $160,000 in interest.

And for the sake of comparison, let's see what happens if Amanda and Michael had ended up with an interest rate of 6.5% over 30 years. In that case, they'd end up paying the bank about $306,000 in interest by the time their home is paid off.

Interestingly, it hasn't always been this way.

Say Helen and William were looking to buy a home prior to The Great Depression. Back then, a mortgage typically required a 50% down payment and the remaining 50% had to be paid off at the end of a 5- or 10-year term. If they paid off their home that fast, can you imagine how much they'd save on interest payments?

Anyhow, back to Amanda and Michael. Say they decided instead to pay off that home in only 15 years. With a 3.75% interest rate, they'd pay around $74,000 in interest, saving them about $85,000! At a 6.5% interest rate, they'd pay around $136,000 in interest — this is a savings of over $165,000 compared to dragging it out over 30 years.

As you can see, the savings are enormous. Imagine what you could do with that amount of extra money waiting for you in your bank account!

Home Purchase Price	$300,000			
Down Payment	$60,000			
	3.75% Interest Rate		6.5% Interest Rate	
Amortization Period	30 years	15 years	30 years	15 years
Monthly Payment	$1,110	$1,740	$1,500	$2,080
Total Interest Paid	$160,000	$74,000	$306,000	$136,000

And if paying off your current home in 15 years (or less!) would cause the payments to be too high, then consider selling your current home and using the proceeds to buy a less expensive home instead. Maybe then you'll be able to afford to pay that sucker off within 15 years or less.

Take a few moments right now to imagine how it would feel to be mortgage-free within 15 years or less.

Seriously. Imagine it right now.

Don't worry yet about how you'll do it. Just imagine how it would feel to accomplish that and how your financial life would improve if you were living in a mortgage-free home. Imagine how it would feel to know that you owned an asset of significant value, and didn't owe a dime to anyone for it.

Did you do it? Could you see that scenario in your mind's eye?

I hope so. And if you can't, take the time to think long and hard about it until you can imagine it clearly.

Because whenever you want to accomplish something that seems difficult, it'll be much easier if you're 100% clear on why you're doing it and exactly what you're going to get out of it. That, my friend, can give you the motivation you need to keep going when things get tough. I call this "keeping your eye on the prize".

So don't fall into the trap of assuming that you ought to go with a 30-year mortgage when you can save so much cash by paying off your home sooner.

If you're thinking about how on earth you'd be able to afford to do it, keep reading.

Before you decide that you can't afford to pay off your house fast, you've got to take the time to learn where every single penny that you earn is going. Because that's the only way to be 100% certain whether or not you really can, or cannot, afford to pay off a house in 15 years — or maybe even sooner!

Who knows, you might be pleasantly surprised by how far your money can stretch if you make more strategic spending decisions.

Whatever you do, don't let budgeting your money intimidate you — it's easy to do. The trick is to track what you're spending, track what you're earning, and plan ahead for things that you need to save up for (such as yearly insurance premium payments, yearly property tax payments, etc.).

You can keep things simple by jotting all this down in a notebook, and adding up the figures with your calculator. Or, if you're savvy with spreadsheets, make yourself a budget tracker.

I've got to tell you. Budgeting your money is absolutely 100% mandatory here. If you have a knack for it, great — get started today.

If you're turned off or overwhelmed by the idea of budgeting your money…

And if budgeting isn't your strong suit, then get help. If you like my style, I humbly suggest that you try out my other book, *How to Stop Living Paycheck to Paycheck.* It'll tell you everything you need to know about how to set up a budget that takes only 15 minutes a week, and it even includes a free download for my wickedly good budgeting tool, the Money Tracker.

Or, check out someone else's book. Either way, get the help you need to put an end to budget-overwhelm.

Okay? Good. Then let's move on.

Now it's time to move on to one of the most common myths that adds fuel to the fire for a 30-year mortgage. You don't want to get burned, so keep reading.

LIE! You should keep your mortgage because you get an income tax deduction

I die a little inside every time I hear someone repeat this myth. Man oh man.

Anyhow, to show you exactly why the income tax deduction isn't a good reason to keep your mortgage, you're going to have to stick with me as I go through some calculations here.

Say you buy a $300,000 home. You make a 20% down payment. You end up with a mortgage of $240,000 that you plan on paying off over 30 years. Your interest rate over the next five years is 3.5%.

Your monthly payments are going to be around $1075/month ($12,900 total in 12 months). The amount of that that goes towards interest payments is about $690/mo — a whopping $8280 total in 12 months.

Now let's pretend that you either saved up, or lucked out and came into a windfall of cash that you could use to pay off your mortgage in full.

Are you better off paying it off to save on all that interest you're paying to the bank? Or should you keep the mortgage to get the income tax deduction from the interest you're paying?

Well, let's run the numbers and see.

Let's carry on with our game of pretend, and pretend that you pay 25% of your earnings to the IRS for income tax.

If you paid off your mortgage, you'd no longer have to pay $8280 of your earnings to the bank in the form of interest charges. Instead, you'd be paying the IRS income tax on that $8280, and if you're in the 25% tax bracket, you'd pay the IRS $2070.

So what's better? Giving the bank the full $8280? Or paying the IRS only $2070?

Obviously you're way better off if you pay off your mortgage, and save all that money that you'd otherwise have been paying to the bank, right?

Hell, even if you're in the highest tax bracket, paying about 40% of your income in taxes, you're still way better off paying off your mortgage. Because paying the IRS 40% of $8280 ($3312 in taxes) is still a lot better than paying 100% of $8280 to the bank.

So I rest my case. Do not ever, ever, ever make the mistake of thinking that you're saving money by not paying off your mortgage.

Want to do some calculations that are specific to where you live? No problem. Here's a handy know mortgage calculator that estimates exactly how much you'll save on taxes each year by carrying a mortgage, and allows you to compare that figure to how much you'll be paying each year in interest payments.

http://www.bankrate.com/calculators/mortgages/loan-tax-deduction-calculator.aspx

LIE! You should keep your mortgage because interest rates are lower than other types of loans and you can invest the money in the stock market or a mutual fund

Proponents of this idea say it's the way to go because the amount of interest you're paying on the mortgage is offset by the profits you'll make from investing the money in a good mutual fund or similar investment.

Before you jump all over this, do some quick math and see if it's really worth the risk to you. Because the odds are high that it isn't worth the risk at all.

Let's say you saved up $10,000 cash and are debating whether or not to use it to pay down your mortgage where you're paying 3.5% interest or invest it in a mutual fund where you're told to expect an 7.5% return.

If you use it to pay down your mortgage, you'll save $350 (i.e. 3.5% of $10,000).

If the mutual fund prediction is correct, you'll make $750 in profit. So that's $400 more than what you would have saved if you'd put it down on your mortgage.

But we didn't take into account income taxes yet. Let's say this $750 profit is taxed at a 20% capital gains rate. If that's the case, you'll pay the IRS $150, and have $600 left over to enjoy.

So now you're only $250 ahead of where you'd be if you'd put that $10,000 cash towards paying down your mortgage (i.e. $600 profit from investment - $350 savings on mortgage interest = $250).

Maybe that sounds like a good trade to you. But there's one more thing you need to consider.

Risk.

If you put that $10,000 towards your mortgage (3.5% interest), it's a 100% guarantee that you save $350.

But if instead you put that $10,000 into that mutual fund, it's not a guarantee that you'll end up having $600 in after-tax profit to enjoy.

The market could tank.

The prediction of the return you'll get could be wrong. Maybe the mutual fund only ends up making you $300 in after-tax profit. If that happened, you would have been $50 further ahead if you'd put the 10 grand towards paying down your mortgage.

Who knows! Anything could happen.

So unless you're a long-term, time-tested, exceptional stock or investment fund picker, I recommend that you put that $10,000 cash towards your mortgage.

LIE! There's nothing wrong with buying furniture, vacations, or electronics with a loan

Here's the thing. Every single one of these things will go down, down, down in value starting the very second you take them home, and you risk owing more than it's worth from day one. (Okay, so you can't take your vacation home, but you get the idea. Once you take that trip, you can't sell it to recoup any of your money.)

If you're ever tempted to add to your debt by using credit to buy furniture, a vacation, a new TV, or some other big-ticket electronic item, stop yourself immediately and remind yourself of the cold, hard facts.

1. Financing these things with debt almost always means you'll pay more for it. The next time you're tempted to finance something like this with debt, calculate how much extra it'll cost you once you take into account all the interest and fees you'll pay.

2. You don't need any of these things. You won't die, get sick, or have any other horror fall upon you if you don't buy it.

Disliking your current furniture is no excuse. The fact that the upholstery is wearing out isn't either (because you can patch it yourself or cover it with a blanket/cover until you've saved up the cash to replace it).

No one needs a new TV, home entertainment system, stereo, home automation system, smart phone or even a computer — humans survived for eons without these things.

Maybe you're shocked that I include a computer on that list since I make my living with one. But I can assure you that's only because I could save up cash to buy one in the first place. Until then, I made do without one. And you can too.

If you need to type up a resume, or a letter, for example, you can simply head over to your local library and do it there. Or ask a friend or family member if you can borrow their computer. Even if you consider the cost of giving them money for the paper and ink used to print your letter or resume, the cost is still far less than that of buying your own computer.

If you need to do some online research, most local libraries will allow you to do this for free.

Now on to the topic of vacations. "But I need it to relieve my stress!" some might say. The truth is, there are plenty of ways to relieve stress for free. Local libraries have loads of books on the topic of stress relief — you can learn about using meditation, exercise, and all kinds of other things to relieve stress. And they cost absolutely nothing. Don't get me wrong, I'm certainly not opposed to vacations. But you have to be able to afford them in order to take them. If you can't afford it and take out a loan to pay for it, you'll only add MORE stress to your life due to the payments you'll be making long after the fun has ended.

3. If you need to finance it with debt, you can't afford it. Period. There are no ands, ifs or buts that will ever make financing this kind of thing with debt a wise decision.

4. Even no-money-down, no-interest loans are risky. You see, usually these kinds of so-called "deals" come with a catch. Maybe it's a no-payments-for-one-year deal — but part of the deal is that if for any reason you aren't able to pay it off before the 1 year is up, you'll be slapped with extremely high interest rates until you do.

LIE! Car loans are unavoidable if you want to own a car

> *"If you think nobody cares if you're alive, try missing a couple of car payments."* Earl Wilson

In this section, you'll gain a great deal of clarity on the issues surrounding borrowing money to buy a car, so I highly recommend that you read this section carefully.

First, if you live and work (or go to school) in an urban area with public transit, most people can get by without a car. Taking public transit is often inconvenient, sure. But it'll save you a ton of cash compared to making car payments.

Now I'm <u>not</u> saying that everyone with access to public transit shouldn't own a car.

The point I'm getting at is that if the only way you can afford to buy a car right now is by getting a car loan, and you have access to public transit for getting to work or school, there's a good chance that you should not be buying that car.

I hope you're not getting annoyed at me for saying that. Stick with me a minute or so longer.

Brent lives in Chicago and is debating whether or not to buy a car via a loan. If he buys a monthly public transit pass, it'll cost him 100 bucks a month. But he feels that given his decent job and the fact that everyone else in his social circle has a car, he should have one too. He feels social pressure to conform. And besides, taking public transit to get to his job every day means a longer commute.

Scenario A

If he buys a brand new 2016 Honda Civic LX, it'll cost him $19,670 by the time taxes and fees are added on.

His bank told him they'll give him a car loan at 4% interest, to be paid off over 60 months (five years). His monthly payments will be $362. When the car is paid off, he'll have paid the bank a total of $21,720, or $2050 more compared to paying cash.

Brent isn't rich, so to him, having an extra $2050 would be a lot of money.

But wait, there's more. Brent works downtown, so if he drives a car to work every day, he'll have to pay $180 per month to park his vehicle there. He also has to insure his car. That will cost him close to $100 a month. And last, but not least, he'll be responsible for maintenance and repairs. He's budgeting low for this since it's a brand new car under warranty - he figures $400/year is a good number (works out to $33 per month. He also budgets $200 per month for gas.

So the grand total cost of car ownership if he gets a loan to buy it comes out to $875/month (=$362 + $180 + $100 + $33 + $200).

Over the next five years, assuming all his estimates were accurate, he'll spend $52,500 for the convenience of buying that car, using financing.

Now it's time to consider how this new car purchase will look if he does it another way.

Scenario B

He can use public transit for a grand total of $100/month.

For the purposes of this example, let's say Brent could afford to pay $875 per month to own a car if he really wanted to.

But let's say he decides to suck it up and use public transit while he saves up the difference in cost to buy the car in cash. How long will it take?

Well, by taking public transit, he can set aside $775 per month (i.e. $875 cost of car ownership - $100 cost of using public transit). In only 26 months, he'll have saved up $20150. Even if the cost of a new vehicle goes up by then, he'll still only have to save for one or two more months, at most.

So let's see how the numbers look now:

26 months of public transit at $100 per month adds up to $2600.

Buying the car with cash cost him $20,150. (For the purposes of this example, let's assume that two years from now, a brand new Honda Civic LX would cost that amount, including all taxes and fees.)

Then we'll tack on another 34 months of car ownership expenses, which would be about $17,442 (i.e. $180/mo parking fee + $100/mo insurance + $33/mo average repairs + $200/mo gas).

The grand total he'll spend on transportation costs over the next 60 months (5 years) if he uses public transit for the first 26 months while he saves up to buy that car in cash is $40,192.

By choosing to save up and buy that car in cash, he's basically putting an extra 12 thousand dollars in his pocket. (i.e. $52,500 - $40,192)

Poof!

Just like that.

So what was the point of all that?

To show you how much money a person can save by using public transit while they save up cash to buy a car, and to show how quickly one can save up the cash to buy a car outright (even a brand new one!) if one makes strategic spending decisions.

Are you rich enough to basically burn 12 thousand bucks just so you can have a brand new car today?

And maybe you don't want to buy a brand new car. Which is a good thing, actually. Because you can save more cash by buying a good quality used vehicle.

Scenario C

Let's say our friend Brent from Chicago decides to buy a used Honda Civic that's in excellent shape. He has to save up some cash first, and after 10 months of taking public transit he has $7750 saved up (i.e. $775 x 10 months). He finds a really nice used Honda Civic LX for sale with an asking price of $7750.

Because it's not a brand new vehicle, he budgets more for repairs -

about $1200/year, which works out to $100 per month if you average it out. He adds in $180/mo for parking downtown, $100/mo for insurance, and $200/mo for gas. The grand total works out to $580/mo.

So what does this add up to over 5 years?

10 months of public transit costs him $1000.

The car cost him $7750 to buy.

And 50 months of driving the car cost him $29,000.

That all adds up to $37,750.

So in this scenario where he saves up for a quality used car, he's putting an extra $14,750 in his pocket compared to buying a brand new Honda Civic LX today via a car loan for 100% of the cost. (i.e. $52,500 - $37,750).

Now obviously many of these numbers are best guesses. But a best guess is better than no guess at all and blindly signing up for a five-year car loan.

This is the kind of number crunching you need to do before you assume that you have to borrow money to purchase a vehicle. Look at the alternatives. Calculate the costs. See if the savings are worthwhile (usually, they are!)

LIE! Leasing a car is cheap and affordable

Oh man, don't get me started on leasing a car. Leasing a vehicle is often thought of as a more sophisticated way of owning one. And some people spout over-simplified nonsense such as "always rent or lease things that go down in value". If you've ever heard that kind of crazy talk, this section of the book is for you. You'll never again be left feeling unsure about leasing, wondering if you're missing out by not doing it.

Let's go back to Brent and that Honda Civic LX he wants.

The dealership tells him he can drive away a brand new Honda Civic LX for only $165/mo including tax. The lease term is 36 months (three years).

By the way, there's also a one-time fee for title and licensing of $170, and a one-time document fee of $600.

Err, how about no.

In three years he'll lease another new car, and for the sake of simplicity and our rough estimate, let's pretend the fees and price remain the same. That means another one-time fee for title and licensing of $170, and a one-time document fee of $600.

The total cost of leasing for the next five years will be $11,440.

Don't forget to tack on $180 per month for parking downtown for work, $100 a month for insurance, $33/mo for maintenance and repairs, plus $200/mo for gas. All that adds up to $513/mo, or $30780 over five years.

The grand total for leasing that vehicle is $42,220 (i.e. $11,440 + $30780).

Okay, so maybe now you're thinking that doesn't look too bad.

DON'T BE FOOLED. Car dealerships want you to think that. It's all part of their master plan.

Now keep reading.

We already know that Scenario A, getting a loan to finance the purchase of a new car, is an expensive way to go, so I'm not even going to bother comparing leasing to that.

Instead, let's compare leasing to the better options of Scenario B and C.

In Scenario B, Brent saves up the cash to buy a brand new car after using public transit for a couple of years.

The cost of his transportation for five years ends up being $40,192. So already, it's cheaper than leasing, although not by a huge amount of money.

But since Civics are well-made and tend to be reliable, he figures he'll keep this car for 10 years, no problem.

For Scenario B, let's add up the cost of his transportation for 10 years (which includes 26 months of public transit while he saves up the cash to buy the car, 60 months of low $33/mo repair costs because the car is under warranty, and 34 months of higher $100/mo repair costs after that).

For years 6-10 he'll spend $10,800 ($180/mo) on parking downtown, $6000 ($100/mo) for insurance, and $12,000 ($200/mo) for gas. Car maintenance will cost him $4258 (i.e. 26 months at the new car warranty rate of $33/mo plus 34 months at the older car no warranty rate of $100/mo). All of that adds up to $33,058.

So if he saves up the cash to buy a brand new Honda Civic, and keeps it for 10 years, he'll pay a total of $73,250 for owning and operating that vehicle.

And, now this is important, he still owns the vehicle and could sell it for cash if he wanted. Say he sold it for $6500. Now his costs of transportation over the past 10 years drops to only $66,750 (i.e. $73,250 - $6500 profit from selling the car).

Whereas if he leases a new vehicle every three years, he'll pay the fees that come with the start of a new lease three times in a 10 year period, for a total of $2310. And he'll pay 10 years worth of monthly lease payments, totaling $19,800. And he'll pay 10 years worth of parking fees, gas, insurance, plus maintenance and repairs (at the new car rate), for a total of $61,560.

That brings the cost of leasing a vehicle for 10 years to about $83,670.

Leasing a Honda Civic for 10 years would cost Brent about $17,000 more than he'd spend on transportation if he bought it brand new for cash.

And as you'll remember, Brent would save even more money under Scenario C where he buys a high quality used Honda Civic for cash.

Repeat after me. "Leasing a car instead of buying a high quality vehicle for cash will almost always cost more money in the long run."

Never, ever, lease a vehicle unless you've taken the time to calculate the true costs, compared it to reasonable alternatives, and proven to yourself that it'll save you money.

LIE! All loans with collateral are good debt

I came across an interesting discussion the other day where someone was arguing that any loan that has collateral is actually good debt, because you can pay it off anytime you want by selling the collateral used to obtain the loan in the first place.

This is such complete and utter nonsense that you should be recoiling from the very idea of it. Here's why.

First, the value of the collateral could go down and leave you with a loan for more money than you can get from selling said collateral.

And second, if the loan isn't making you more money than what you're paying in interest, it's basically causing you to flush your hard-earned money down a virtual toilet due to all the interest you're paying to the bank (which you'd never have to pay if you'd bought the thing with cash in the first place).

You work hard for your money. Don't flush it down a virtual toilet for no good reason.

Summing up

Now you know enough not to be fooled by the lies you've been told about debt. It's now time to sort out the good debt from the bad so you can prioritize what to pay off first. The next chapter will tell you how to do that.

Good Debt Versus Bad Debt

"Some debts are fun when you're acquiring them, but none are fun when you set about retiring them."
Ogden Nash

While some people believe that all debt is bad, I'm not one of them.

But.

Most of the debts that the average person has are not the good kind and can destroy your dreams of financial freedom so fast it'll make your head spin.

It'll be well worth your time to keep reading and gain clarity on how to tell the difference between good and bad debt, so you can avoid the kind that'll hurt you. And if you already have bad debts, it'll be much clearer to you why you need to get rid of them.

The 3 criteria that all good debt needs to meet

In order for debt to be good, it needs to meet ALL three of the following criteria:

1. It makes you more money than what it's costing you to have it.
2. It has high odds of turning a profit.
3. It's money that you can afford to lose.

(If it only meets one, or even two of them, it's bad debt.)

Here are some examples and details to illustrate what I mean.

1. re: It makes you more money than what it's costing you to have it.

A classic example of this is borrowing money at 2% interest to invest in something that makes you a 10% profit. After paying the 2% interest to the bank, plus any taxes you owe on your profit, you end up with more money than you started out with.

2. re: It has high odds of turning a profit.

Say you're expecting to make a 10% profit with borrowed money by investing in the stock market. What are the odds of your prediction coming true? What are the odds of you losing all the money in the market and having to pay back the bank with your personal cash?

In many (if not most) cases, the risk involved doesn't make the potential profits worth the costs of borrowing the money, so such a debt would not count as good debt.

Obviously it's a judgment call as to whether or not the odds of making a profit are any good. To make your predictions as accurate as possible you should gather as much research as you can, run the numbers for various potential scenarios, and make your best call.

3. re: It's money that you can afford to lose.

That is, you can afford to pay it off on your own even if you lose all the borrowed money that you tried to invest. Because if you can't afford to pay off the debt on your own, you probably shouldn't have it in the first place. This may sound overly strict, but if you take this into consideration the next time you consider signing up for some "good debt", it can save you from a world of hurt if your investment doesn't yield the expected profits, or worse, ends up losing all the money you borrowed.

So for the rest of this chapter, we're going to look at debt using the above criteria to classify it as either good or bad debt.

Remember, good debt is borrowed money that's making you more cash than the cost of carrying the debt, has dramatically good odds of making profits worth the risk of borrowing the money in the first place, and that you can pay off on your own if necessary (ex. if you lose all the borrowed money due to your investment going bad).

It really is that simple.

The focus of this book is specifically on getting rid of bad debts. Because those are the ones that are mostly likely to get in your way of a life free from worries about money. They should be avoided if possible, and if you have them, you should consider the task of getting rid of them to be urgent.

On the flip side, in certain situations, good debt can be a useful tool for growing one's wealth more quickly and might be worth the risk of taking on. But that's a topic for another book. Please note that I said "in certain situations" and "might". And I certainly am not suggesting that good debt is free of risk.

In any case, before I go on, let's take a look at a couple of examples to make it clear what the differences are between good and bad debt.

An example of good debt

Because our criteria for good debt takes into account what you can afford to lose (and everyone will be different), there isn't a one-size-fits-all rule. However, the example that follows will help you to see how we can evaluate debt to figure out if it's good or bad.

And because it's the details that make all the difference, those are included too.

Michael is 45 years old. He paid off his house, which is worth about $300,000 in today's market. He rents out two spare bedrooms in his home to local college students, which earns him $12,000 per year.

He earns $36,000 a year from his pension. (Yes, he's young to have a pension... but he had a job at the local jail that he started when he was 19 years old. After 25 years, he decided to take early retirement and collect his pension.)

He also works full-time mowing neighborhood lawns. He's built up quite a large list of regular customers over the years and earns $48,000 a year doing that.

He's single with no dependents. He's in perfect health. He has solid insurance policies to cover him if he becomes unable to work due to a serious illness or disability.

Michael wants to bump up his retirement nest egg, so he buys a condo for $187,500 that's in excellent condition to rent out. He puts a $37,500 down payment on the condo, leaving him with a $150,000 mortgage that's scheduled to be paid off in 20 years. If he adds up his property taxes, home owner association fees, expected maintenance/repairs and mortgage payments, he'd need to bring in a minimum of $1650 per month to break even in terms of cash flow.

Because this condo is in a high demand neighborhood with ridiculously low vacancy rates, he's able to get $1650 per month in rent. His plan is to manage the property himself, and because he's a handy guy, he can handle simple maintenance issues on his own.

Let's assess his condo debt to see if it's good or bad debt.

For the purposes of this example, I'm going to calculate the return on his investment for the next five years only.

Please note that the best calculation would be for a long-term projection of what would happen if he owned this property for 20 years. The longer he holds onto this property, the greater his returns are likely to be since in the early years a very large percentage of his mortgage payment is going towards interest, whereas in the later years of his mortgage a larger percentage is going towards the principal. Additionally, holding on to the property long-term protects him from short-term fluctuations in value.

Anyhow, here we go.

In the first five years of ownership, an average of a little over $26,000 of the condo's mortgage is going to be paid off. And since historically speaking, the rate of home price appreciation approximately matches the rate of inflation (if you take into account the increase in home sizes over the same time period), I'm going to assume he makes nothing from appreciation.

Important note: For the record, I don't advise you to invest in real estate if you only plan on keeping the property for five years. Due to the potential for short-term volatility in the market, you have greater odds of taking a horrible loss. On the flip side, if you buy with the intention of holding onto it for 20 years or more, the odds are extremely high that you'll make a profit if you buy the right property. Of course, there's a lot more to it than that — and there are too many details to go into here. But do keep this fact in mind.

Okay, so he put in $37,500 of his own money (for the down payment), and not a penny more. The rent covered all other expenses. So the debt is paying for itself. (Criteria #1 for good debt is met.)

And say the housing market was flat, and the property value didn't increase at all when considering inflation. Even then, he'd have made a good return on his investment. (Criteria #2 is met.)

Here are the quick and dirty calculations that allowed me to arrive at that conclusion.

[$26,000 (amount of mortgage paid off)/$37,500]100/5 years = 13% return on his investment per year.

This debt is making him more money than what it's costing him to have it, the odds are good that it will continue to do, and worst case scenario he can afford to pay it off on his own without declaring bankruptcy.

Even if home prices fell by 50% a year after bought it, he couldn't find a good tenant so was now missing out on rental income, and he wanted to get out, he could sell the condo and his house, pay off the mortgage, and be debt free. Poof. Just like that. Sure, it would really stink to have to do that since he'd lose money, but if push came to shove, he could afford to pay off the debt on his own. (Criteria #3 for good debt.)

For the above reasons, I consider his mortgage on the rental condo to be good debt, and not as urgent to pay off.

Paying off bad debt, on the other hand, should always be considered an urgent matter. The very facts that it doesn't pay for itself and doesn't generate profits means you're at greater risk of it someday causing you undo financial hardship compared to good debt.

Please note: After more urgent financial matters have been attended to, it's definitely worth considering paying off your good debts as soon as possible. Because the less debt you have, the less risk you're exposed to.

Examples of bad debt

Michael's friend Frank suggests that he buy a lakefront cabin in the woods to have as a fun place to escape to on the weekends. This would require him to take out a 20-year mortgage for $300,000.

He says Michael deserves it, and the extra space would be nice.

The trouble is, Michael wouldn't be making any money off it.

The interest rate being charged on the mortgage is 4%. Once again, since historically speaking, the rate of home price appreciation approximately matches the rate of inflation (if you take into account the increase in home sizes over the same time period), I'm going to assume he makes nothing from appreciation. (If you want to nerd out with me doing the calculations that brought me to this conclusion, please check it out in the Appendix.)

Over the next five years, it'll cost him $54,378 in interest payments.

It'll cost him a total of $17,500 in property taxes ($3500/year x 5 years).

And he figures that he'd spend about $7,500 in maintenance and repairs ($1500/year x 5 years).

If he sells in five years, he'll have spent a total of $79,378 to own it (i.e. $54,378 in interest payments, $17,500 for property taxes, and $7,500 for maintenance/repairs).

Or, to put it another way, assuming he sells it in five years, it would have burned through about $3307 per month that he'll never get back.

Is that worth it? Probably not, unless he can afford to burn that much money a month on a vacation home, *and* plans on spending more than $3307 every single month for five years renting vacation homes on his weekends off (in which case buying it *might* save him some money).

Remember, historically speaking, if you hold onto a piece of real estate for a long period of time and take into account inflation, real estate doesn't actually make you a return on your investment via appreciation. Sure, you can get lucky and make money via appreciation via short term volatility in the market if it works in your favor, but it would be irresponsible to depend on appreciation as the primary way of making money via real estate whether it be your family home, or an investment property.

All that being said, if he holds onto the property for longer than five years, his average monthly interest cost will go down with time (because the longer you make payments on a mortgage, the lower the percentage of your payment that goes towards interest). Ultimately, the only way to know for sure if it's "worth it" to buy will depend on Michael's preferences and how long he plans on keeping it. But for anyone who holds onto such a vacation home short term, as you saw, it's often not worth it at all.

An intelligence upgrade from following the herd?

Sometimes following the herd is a good thing. It saves us the time of figuring out what to do on our own. We use the wisdom of the crowd to our benefit. It can provide us with an intelligence upgrade because we can base our decisions on the pooled knowledge of the group as a whole, rather than just our own relatively small slice of it.

But other times, it doesn't work out so great. Not just for us mere mortals, but for animals too.

The Daily Mail reported on the case of 28 cows that, possibly spooked by thunderstorms, ran off a cliff one after the other and died.

USA Today reported the baffling case of almost 2000 sheep in Turkey who did the same thing. The first 450 to jump ended up dead.

Can you imagine such a thing? It's insanity!

I bet those animals regretted following the herd the second they hit bottom.

We like to think that as humans, we're smarter than that. But sometimes our human herd makes the wrong call too.

And unfortunately, many members of our herd are big time into credit card debt.

Credit card debt is rotten to the core and you need to get rid of it

For the purposes of our discussion, credit card debt is the amount of money you owe to a credit card company that you do not pay off in full each month.

And it's pretty much always bad debt because it's usually used to purchase things that won't turn a profit (ex. clothes, furniture, entertainment, dining out etc.).

On top of that, it's one of the highest-interest methods of borrowing money. Credit card interest rates can be as high as 30% — or more! Whereas at the time of this writing lines of credit can be had from the bank for less than 5% if you have good credit.

The scary thing is that according to an [American Bankers Association May 2016 report](), 42.1% of American credit card accounts have balances that are not paid off in full each month.

And it gets more scary if we ignore the accounts that aren't being used, because then it's just over 58.6% of active accounts are not paid off each month, compared to 49.4% that are.

So I ask you this.

Would you rather be one of the minority that saves big bucks on interest charges by paying off your credit card in full each month?

Or would you rather follow the herd off a financial cliff, joining the ones that don't pay theirs off every month?

Obviously the ideal situation is for you avoid going over that cliff to begin with.

But keep in mind that *worst case, even if you've already gone over that cliff, you can fix it.* That's what this book is all about, after all. Remember that, okay?

> *"Money often costs too much."* Ralph Waldo Emerson

Think about this for a moment.

If you carry a $10,000 balance on a credit card with an interest rate of 12% you're paying $1200 per year in interest. If the interest rate is 30%, you're paying $3000 per year in interest.

Now if that's your situation, don't let the knowledge of how much money is being wasted on interest discourage you.

Instead, use this knowledge to light a fire under you that fuels your determination to put an end to the madness now.

You can pay it off.

You really can.

You just have to start, and take it one step at a time.

Other kinds of bad debt

As you can imagine, loans used to buy things like furniture, a vehicle, vacations and electronics all fall into the bad debt category, should be considered urgent, and should be paid off as soon as possible. All of these things go down in value with time, and aren't likely to generate income for you that will offset what you're paying in interest on their loans.

Your goal for bad debt

Your number one goal for bad debt is to get rid of it as soon as humanly possible. This kind of debt is the equivalent of setting your money on fire every single day (what a waste!), and it's needlessly increasing the financial risk you're exposing yourself to if you can't afford to pay it off right now.

Action Steps

1. It's time for a reality check. Because you can't fix what you don't know is broke.

Right now, I want you to go through every credit card, every bank statement, every loan statement, every single bill you have, and find out how much debt you have.

Don't let it depress you. Don't let it get you down.

And although it may not feel this way, you're tougher than that, starting now. You're going to be an action taker, a doer. And you're going to fix this.

And if by some chance it's late at night…

… and you worry that doing this now will keep you awake all night, go to your calendar and set aside some time to do this within the next 24 hours. I'm serious. This is immensely important if you want to get control over your debt — you need to create the time to do this.

2. Create a chart so the info is easy to read and well-organized. For every single one of your debts, write down the following information:

- what the debt is for (ex. Car loan, credit card, furniture loan etc.)
- who you owe it to (ex. MasterCard, Bank of America line of credit, Ford dealership car loan etc.)
- the interest rate
- the minimum payment due each month
- the remaining balance owing
- classify it as good or bad debt based on the three criteria discussed in this chapter.

To make this job faster and easier, I've created a tool to track it all for you: The Debt Destroyer. If you'd like to get your hands on it, go here to get it:
https://averybreyer.com/your-road-to-wealth-starts-here-1/

3. Whatever you do, don't freak out when you see the totals. Give yourself a pat on the back for keeping it real and facing your debt head on. This is the first step to destroying it once and for all.

4. Put this info aside for now. You'll find out how to handle it in the upcoming chapters.

Summing up

I'm pretty hard core when it comes to getting rid of bad debt. That's why we paid off our home in under five years. That's why aside from the first vehicle I ever bought right after graduating with my university degree (which I should have saved up to buy without a loan, mind you), every single vehicle I've ever bought has been paid for in cash. And I avoid credit card debt like the plague.

Look, if you can't sell everything and pay it all off right this minute, your bad debt is a massive freaking emergency and needs to be paid off as soon as humanly possible.

And if you could theoretically sell everything you own to pay off your bad debts, but it would cause you undue hardship to do so, it's merely a regular emergency. But seriously, do you really want to live with a potential financial emergency every single day? I think not.

Truly, if you have bad debts, you need to get rid of them asap. Period. And that will open up a world of possibilities for growing your wealth and creating a prosperous financial future.

Next, we're going to talk about mortgages and whether it's good or bad debt. It's typically one of the largest debts that any of us ever have, so it's important to stick it in the right category so you know what to do about it.

P.S. If you're renting, you still need to read this chapter. Because the conclusions drawn about how much of a monthly mortgage payment is affordable also applies to monthly rent.

Mortgages

"Home is where the heart is." Pliny the Elder

Mortgages deserve their own chapter because they are one of the largest monthly expenses that most people spend money on, and involve a commitment to pay X amount of money over a long period of time, often as long as three decades.

Is your mortgage a good or bad debt?

It can be either, depending on your circumstances.

Here's a quick reminder of the three criteria that all good debts must meet:

1. It makes you more money than what it's costing you to have it, **and**...
2. It has high odds of turning a profit, **and**...
3. It's money that you can afford to lose.

Now we'll take a look at a couple of examples to illustrate the difference between a mortgage that's good debt and a mortgage that's bad debt.

Example 1

Sara has saved up $60,000 cash and is debating whether or not she ought to avoid taking on a mortgage and just continue to rent a house, or if she ought to buy one.

She plans on living in the same home for at least 20 years — all of her family is in this town, there are lots of jobs, and she loves the area. In other words, if she buys, she'll be holding onto the property for the long term, which makes it very likely that her home would be worth more than what she paid for it by the time she's ready to consider selling.

She's currently paying $1850 per month to rent a house. Utilities are not included.

She could buy a comparable home for $300,000. If she puts a $60,000 down payment towards it, and gets a 30-year mortgage at 4% interest, her monthly mortgage payments will be about $1140 per month. Additional expenses that she'll have to take on that she didn't have to worry about when renting include the following:

- Property taxes
- Maintenance and repairs

For the purposes of our example, Sara's property taxes are expected to be $3000 per year, which averages out to $250/month.

And she's budgeting 1.5% of her home's value for maintenance and repairs each year, which averages out to $375 per month (i.e. [300,000 x 0.015]/12)

So now we're looking at a total of about $1765 per month in housing expenses if she buys a house (i.e. $1140 mortgage payment + $250 property taxes + $375 maintenance and repairs = $1765).

Given this situation, the odds are good that she's better off buying compared to renting.

Aside from the obvious break-even on monthly expenses, the really big advantage of buying is that 20 years from now, she'll have paid off about $187,000 worth of the purchase price (with $113,000 left to pay off).

Assuming that housing prices go up at approximately the rate of inflation (see Appendix, 4% is a decent estimate for average annual inflation), her home will be worth about $657,336 at that time. So if she sells, she'll pocket about $544,000 before taking into account any realtor commissions or other expenses incurred when selling her home.

Whereas if she rented, she'd get nothing.

In this case, her mortgage can be considered to be good debt. In fact, it's a very good debt. The risk is so low and the profit is so large compared to the zero she'd get by renting that buying a home is a no brainer for her.

Criteria 1 is met because she's going to spend the same amount of money on housing whether she buys or rents, and she'll end up making money if she sells 20 years from now as planned.

Criteria 2 is met because given her numbers and the fact that she plans on holding onto the property for 20 years she has high odds of making a profit compared to renting (because it's highly unlikely that her property will be worth less than what she paid for it when she sells).

Criteria 3 is met because she can afford to lose the money. If a freak calamity (ex. natural disaster for which insurance won't cover her) happened that destroyed her home, she could afford to make the mortgage payments in addition to paying rent on a new place to live. Sure, she'd have to downsize dramatically to pull this off, but she could do it.

Example 2

Jim is currently renting. His job transfers him to a new city every 2-3 years. He hates paying rent and is tempted to buy. So he considers the pros and cons.

It turns out that while he can buy a place for the same monthly costs as he's paying in rent, his odds of making a profit aren't good enough to make him pull the trigger.

This is because he's in a city with a volatile real estate market where prices have a history of making large swings over short periods of time. In 2013 prices went up by 15%, in 2014 they went up by 5%, and in 2015 they fell by 20%. Who knows what'll happen this year and next before he'd have to sell.

In this case, buying a condo or house doesn't meet our second criteria for good debt because the risk of losing money if he buys for such a short period of time is too high.

He opts to rent.

On the other hand, if Jim could have bought a well-maintained home and been sure that he'd hold onto it for at least 20 years, the risk of losing money on the purchase would have been next to nothing, because even in a volatile market, over a long period of time the general trend is for housing to go up at approximately the rate of inflation. (You can read more about this in the Appendix.)

Mortgages and you

If you have a mortgage now, or are thinking of getting one in the future, be sure to run the numbers for yourself and determine whether or not a mortgage meets the criteria for good debt in your situation.

We all have a different tolerance for risk. We all have varying incomes. Some people can handle a loss (both financially and emotionally) from buying a home more easily than others. Some people can mitigate any financial risks involved with buying a home (ex. over-budget repairs) by earning more money or cutting expenses. Others can't.

Always calculate the expected expenses and potential profit compared to renting for yourself, weigh the pros and cons of available choices, and make the best decision you can based on your individual financial situation and temperament.

Trailers and Mobile Homes

Although trailers and mobile homes can be used for housing, they're not in the same category as a house or condominium when it comes to being an investment.

This is because unlike houses and condominiums, trailers and mobile homes tend to decrease in value with time, rather than increase. As far as profit potential goes, it's comparable to living in a car.

The exception is if you buy a cheap one for cash that's already lost pretty much all of its value. In other words, when you sell, you figure you'll get all of your money back. If doing so will cost you less than renting, this might be worth it if you want to live really frugally for a few years and save up some cash.

Obviously this doesn't mean that buying a trailer or mobile home is always a bad idea. Just as with anything else, everyone's circumstances are different and there are always nuances to consider.

If buying one of these will save you money and it meets the three criteria for good debt compared to renting, then by all means go for it if it's what you want to do. But if not, it's probably best avoided.

How to know if you can afford to buy a home

Assuming you've come to the conclusion that a mortgage is likely to be a good debt for you, here are some factors to consider when deciding how much to spend.

Because if you over-stretch your finances by taking on mortgage payments that are too high, you'll struggle more than necessary to pay off your bad debts because too much money will be going towards housing.

First, throw out any notion of one-size-fits-all guidelines. Despite claims to the contrary, there aren't any.

For example, it's commonly said that as long as your debt to income ratio isn't greater than 43%, you're doing fine.

Sure, if you're making $150,000 a year, and are reasonably careful with your money, odds are that you can easily afford to spend $64,500 a year (about 43%) of it on a combination of mortgage payments, a car loan, and whatever else you borrowed money for, and still have enough leftover to pay for necessities like food, utility bills, healthcare, and clothing.

But that's not the case for people making lower incomes.

Martha bought a condo in good times, and the mortgage payments are $645 a month. Even though she's a single mom of two kids, it was easy to afford this at the time because she had a decently paying job.

But then she got laid off during a downturn in the economy, and the only job she could find now pays a paltry $18,000 per year.

In theory, since she has no other debts, she should be just fine, right?

Because her mortgage payments (her only debt) only add up to 43% of her income (i.e. $645/mo x 12 months/$18,000 x 100 = 43%)

But Martha's not doing fine at all. She only has $855 per month (pre-tax) leftover to cover basic necessities like food, clothing, utilities, and medical expenses — and she's finding it very difficult to pay for all that for her small family of three.

One-size-fits-all plans are flawed. They fail to account for the differences in disposable income between high and low income earners.

Other flawed rules

Another number that's tossed around a lot is the 30% rule.

This rule originated from the 1969 Brook Amendment to the Housing and Urban Development Act of 1968, which introduced the idea that rent for public housing should be no more than 25% of the family income. In 1981, Congress increased this figure to 30%. Sources say[2] these increases were put into place in the hopes that they'd allow rental property owners to better afford maintenance for their properties.

It's dismaying that the reasoning for the 30% rule had nothing to do with how much the average homeowner could afford, yet it's commonly used as a guideline for determining exactly that.

What craziness!

Even worse, is that this 30% standard is now commonly recommended to home buyers as a one-size-fits-all way of deciding how high of a mortgage payment they can afford.

Don't be fooled

So the next time you come across a one-size-fits-all rule for how much to spend on mortgage payments, look at it with skepticism. For most people, I recommend that you aim to spend LESS than these rules dictate. Spending less will allow you more flexibility with your finances and make it easier to afford a bit of fun in your life.

As for how much less you ought to spend, there's only one way to figure that out. You've got to go back to basics. Track your spending and income. Find out how much of your spending is optional and how much of it is for non-negotiable necessities, including savings. Only then will you know how much you can truly afford to spend on a mortgage (or even rent for that matter!).

How fast should you pay off your home

The less debt you have, the less financial risk you're exposed to. After you've paid off your bad debts, plow the money that's been freed up into getting rid of your mortgage as quickly as possible.

Imagine this.

What if housing prices fall by 50% like they did in many areas back in 2008? And what if jobs dry up and many people, including you, have decided that the best option is to move somewhere else with a better job market?

If your mortgage has been paid off, even if you had to move for a better job market on short notice and sell your home for less than you paid for it, you'll probably be okay (granted, not happy about it, but you certainly won't have to worry about going bankrupt over such a thing). Whereas for someone who hasn't paid off their home, being forced by circumstances to sell during a price crash could be stressful if the balance owing is more than the proceeds generated by selling it.

Action step

If you have a mortgage (or are thinking of getting one) run the numbers, assess the risk, and find out if it meets the three criteria for good debt in your unique situation.

If it does, that's great. But if it doesn't, you need to take action.

What to do if your mortgage is bad debt

If you have a mortgage and come to the conclusion that it's bad debt, you need to get rid of it as soon as possible. Here are some options for doing that:

Consider selling it and cutting your losses now if the following three criteria are met:

- you don't think it's likely that you'll be able to hang onto the home long enough for it to turn a profit compared to renting, and,
- the losses are expected to continue to grow with time, and,
- you won't suffer any negative financial consequences such as bankruptcy if you do so

Consider keeping it and paying it off ASAP if the following two criteria are met:

- selling it would ruin your credit because it would force you to declare bankruptcy (for example, if you owe more on the mortgage than the house is worth and you can't afford to repay the difference to the lender), and,
- you can afford to continue making payments

Remember that if your current mortgage is bad debt, that doesn't mean that would be the case with any and all mortgages.

For example, say your mortgage is bad debt because you accidentally bought a home that required mountains of expensive repairs that killed any hope of ever making a profit over time. If you bought a well-maintained home that only required normal levels of repairs, that could be enough to turn a mortgage into good debt for you.

Or, say your mortgage is bad debt because you bought a home that's too expensive. If you sell it and replace it with a less expensive home, the numbers may work out in your favor this time and turn a profit over the long term compared to renting.

Don't assume all mortgages are good debt, or that all mortgages are bad debt for you. Run the numbers and assess the risk each and every time — every mortgage situation is different, even for the same person.

What to do if your mortgage is good debt

Pay it off as soon as you can, using the Power Pay Off Plan that you'll learn about in a future chapter.

Summing up

There's no one-size-fits-all rule for how much you should spend on a home or how high of a mortgage payment you can afford to make. Rules such as the 43% limit for a debt to income ratio or a 30%-of-gross-income upper limit for mortgage or rent payments should not be accepted as automatically affordable for you personally. Unfortunately, there are no short cuts here. The only way to know for sure what your personal limit should be is to run the numbers. Track your earnings. Track your spending. Make an informed decision about what you can afford after you've gathered all the facts.

Figure out if your mortgage is good or bad debt in your situation, and take action based on that. Everyone is different.

Now that you know the difference between good and bad debt, it's time to find out the best way to pay it off. And that information is what you're going to be reading about in the next chapter.

The Power Pay Off Plan (And How Sam Saved 20 Grand)

"Let him who would enjoy a good future waste none of his present." Roger Babson

I'm about to share with you how choosing the right method of paying off debt could save you over $20,000, require you to put down the same amount of money each month as the wrong method, and allow you to be debt-free six-and-a-half years sooner.

How Sam saved twenty grand

Obviously your debt numbers will be different from Sam's, but the lessons in this story will apply to everyone. Read on and see how big savings can be had under the right circumstances.

Sam accumulated a total of $80,000 in debts and is trying to decide on the best way to pay it all off.

His minimum payments add up to about $1276 per month, and if he sticks with that he'll have everything paid off in 20 years.

But he recently started a side business that's already bringing in an extra $200 a month. His plan is to put that extra cash towards paying down his debts faster — and with the extra money he's earning, he can now put $1476 per month towards debt repayment (i.e. $1276 + $200 = $1476).

A big decision

Sam is facing a choice between two strategies of paying everything off.

A very important point is that no matter which debt repayment plan he chooses, he'll still be putting about $1476 per month towards paying it all off until he's finally debt-free.

The first option he's considering is to tackle his highest interest debts first. In theory, that should be the most cost-effective way of paying down his debts, although he's not sure if the savings will be significant or not.

The second option he's considering is to pay off the smallest debts first. Once those are gone he could move on to tackling the larger and more intimidating ones.

Which option would you choose?

His friends are all telling him that this second option is the way to go. They say it'll feel fabulous to get rid of a new debt every few months — the smaller ones can be paid off more quickly — and they say this series of small wins one after the other will help him to stay motivated enough to continue making payments until he's debt free.

His investment adviser tells him he's heard of people having great success with this method too, and it's known as the Snowball Method of paying down debt.

Sam is thinking that this sounds pretty good. He's really excited to be on the verge of finally doing something to better his finances, and is determined to see this through until the end.

Human nature is a funny thing sometimes

Interestingly, research[3] shows that many people will choose the Snowball Method that Sam's friends and investment adviser are so casually suggesting, even if it hurts us financially.

For some reason, our instinct is to minimize the number of debts that we have to manage. Perhaps this is partly due to the fact that with every debt we pay off, we get rid of another annoying monthly bill that we have to deal with — and that's an attractive outcome in the typical fast-paced, busy, and often stressful modern lifestyle.

But the unfortunate fact is that this can sometimes cost us big bucks.

Time for a bombshell

I like to call the first option — paying off debts with the highest interest rates first — the Power Pay Off Plan.

Luckily for Sam, the loan officer at his bank crunched some numbers and suggested that he consider the Power Pay Off Plan. When Sam found out just how much money he'd save, and how many years earlier he'd be free of debt, he was stunned and horrified that he'd almost chosen a path that would have wasted twenty grand of his hard-earned money.

It turns out that if Sam chooses to use the Power Pay Off Plan he'll be debt-free six-and-a-half years earlier and save over $20,000 compared to using the Snowball Method.

How is that possible?

Here's the lowdown on Sam's debts, including the details that his friends and investment adviser failed to consider — the interest rates on his debts.

Sam has three bank accounts at three different banks. Each of them offered him a line of credit when he opened the account.

He made full use of those lines of credit, maxing them out, and now owes a total of $30,000:

- $11k to Bank of America
- $10k to Charles Schwab Bank
- $9k to Wells Fargo

The interest rate on each of those lines of credit is 4%.

Sam also has two credit cards, each charging him 30% interest on any balances. He's managed to max them both out and now owes $20,000 to his MasterCard and $25,000 to his VISA.

Number crunching time

To keep this example from turning into a mess, I kept things simple. The interest rates on his credit cards are the same, so I can combine the credit card debt into one lump sum for calculation purposes. Ditto for the lines of credit.

And neither his credit card companies or banks will penalize him for paying off these debts sooner than the maximum 20 years allowed in this fictional scenario.

So now that we have those assumptions out in the open, here is how things go down.

The sum of the minimum monthly payments owing on his credit cards is $1065. The sum of the minimum monthly payments owing on his lines of credit is $211. All of his debts are due to be paid off in 20 years at that rate.

The question we're dealing with here is whether or not Sam should put the extra $200 a month he's earning from his side business towards paying down the lines of credit, or the credit cards.

Snowball Method

If Sam chose this method, he'd be kicking himself for a long time after finding out how much money he wasted.

He'd spend 99 months paying $411 a month (total) towards his lines of credit, and $1065 a month (total) towards his credit cards.

At the end of month 99, his lines of credit would be paid off.

He'd spend the next 51 months paying $1476 a month towards his credit cards. (At the end of month 51, his credit card debts would be paid off).

In total, he'd have spent 150 months and $116,031 to pay off those debts.

Power Pay Off Plan

If Sam choses this method, he'll end up debt-free sooner and be twenty thousand dollars richer.

He'll spend 51 months paying $1255 a month (total) towards his credit cards and $211 a month (total) towards his lines of credit.

At the end of month 51, his credit cards are all paid off.

He'll spend another 21 months paying $1476 a month (total) towards his lines of credit.

In total, he'd have spent 72 months and $95,485 to pay off those debts.

Important takeaways

No matter which plan he chose, he'd be putting the same amount towards debt repayment every month: $1476.

But with the Power Pay Off Plan, he ends up paying off his debt six-and-a-half years sooner and saving over $20,000 compared to using the Snowball Method.

What you should do for your BAD debts

The Power Pay Off Plan (paying off the highest interest debts first) is almost always the most cost-effective way to pay off your debts (assuming you won't be charged any outrageous penalties for paying off any of your debts early).

Make a list of all your debts and the interest rates for each one. Find out if you'll be charged a penalty for paying off any of your debts early, and if so, how much it is. Generally, you won't have to worry about this with flexible loans such as credit card debts and lines of credit. But it may be an issue with large loans such as mortgages.

Put the highest interest rate debts at the top of your list, and pay them off first. The only exception to this rule is if the penalty incurred by paying it off early cancels out the interest you'll save. If in doubt, speak with your financial adviser about the most cost effective way to pay down the loan early.

For example, some mortgages allow you to pay off an extra 20% in a lump sum once a year without penalty, whereas if you pay extra each month, you'll have to pay a fee. Other mortgages are open and allow you to pay them off whenever you want (these aren't as common, but they do exist).

Continue paying down your debts — highest interest ones first — until they're all gone.

Create small wins with the Power Pay Off Plan

It goes without saying that you ought to celebrate each and every time you pay off a debt. Reward yourself in some way — this can be as simple as indulging in a banana split at the local ice cream parlor, or something more elaborate. Here are two important characteristics of a good reward:

- It's special enough to act as a motivator
- The reward is affordable and doesn't worsen your debt situation

If you're in the midst of paying off a large debt that will take you many months — or even years — to pay off, you need to create small wins throughout that process. For example, you could keep a close eye on the balance owing and celebrate with a reward every time you pay off another $1000 of your debt.

When the Snowball Method is okay to consider

As I keep saying, one-size-fits-all plans for getting rid of bad debts don't work. We're all different.

But before I continue, I want you to keep in mind the following rule, which shouldn't be broken under any circumstances.

<u>Do not use the Snowball Method unless you've first done the work of calculating how much time and money you'd save by using the Power Pay Off Plan.</u>

You need to know if choosing the Snowball Method will cost you a small amount of money, say $100, or a large amount of money, like $20,000. You need to know if choosing the Snowball Method will mean making monthly payments for an extra month, or years.

Once you've done the above calculations, you'll either think the cost of the Snowball Method is tolerable, or not.

Here are some examples of the kinds of scenarios that may make the costs of the Snowball Method acceptable:

Example 1

Ann has two debts. A high-interest car loan for $5000, and a low-interest line of credit where she only owes $200. She loves the idea of paying off her line of credit quickly because it'll give her a quick debt payoff win. Since it's only $200, paying it off before her car loan isn't going to lead to a significant difference in interest paid compared to using the Power Pay Off Plan. She decides to get rid of her line of credit debt first.

Example 2

Ben has three debts and an extra $300 a month to put towards paying them off ahead of schedule. Here is a list of his debts:

- $2000 owing at 29% interest on his VISA
- $543 owing at 26% interest on his MasterCard
- $11,467 owing at 7% interest on his car loan

If he follows the Power Pay Off Plan, he would pay off his debts in the following order: the $2000 VISA debt (29% interest), then the $543 owing on his MasterCard (26% interest), followed by the $11,467 car loan (7% interest).

However, if he follows the Snowball Method he can get rid of that smaller MasterCard debt in only two months (26% interest), then be rid of the balance owing on his MasterCard (29% interest) a few months later, and end by paying off his car loan (7% interest) within a few years. Because the amounts owing on the first two debts to pay off are relatively small, and the difference in interest rates between them is small, it doesn't cost him much to pay off the lower interest rate MasterCard before the higher interest rate VISA.

Ben decides on the Snowball Method because it won't cost him much extra and he feels that the fast win and feeling of satisfaction he'll get from paying off one of his debts so quickly is worth it.

I'm not going to make a judgement on what's worth it to you. Only you can say that.

Just make sure that if you choose the Snowball Method despite knowing it'll cost you more, you go into it knowing exactly how much that cost will be.

Combine the Snowball Method and Power Pay Off Plan

This is the ultimate strategy if some of your bad debts have the same interest rate because it allows you to get the best of both worlds.

Here's an example to show you why that's so.

Angela has the following debts to deal with:

- $2451 owing on her MasterCard at 19% interest
- $3120 owing on her VISA at 19% interest
- $1645 owing on her American Express card at 19% interest
- $3638 owing on her Sears credit card at $24% interest

She decides to use the Power Pay Off Plan and get rid of her debts by paying them off in order of interest rate, from highest to lowest. This means she has to pay off the Sears card first.

But the remaining three debts have the same interest rate. So she borrows from the Snowball Method and pays them off in order of smallest to largest (i.e. first the American Express, then the MasterCard, and finally the VISA).

She saves on interest by paying off the ones with the highest rates first, and then gets to enjoy small wins as quickly as possible by paying off the remaining debts (same interest rates) from smallest to largest.

What to do about your GOOD debts

After you've paid off your BAD debts, it's time to consider paying off your good debts too. But before doing so, you need to consider whether or not paying them off is the best use of your money.

For example, if you put your extra cash into some other investment, would you be further ahead than you'd be by using it to pay off your good debt? The only way to tell is to do the math and see how the numbers shake out.

Another consideration is whether or not you simply want the financial peace of knowing that ALL of your debts (good and bad) are gone. This may make it worth it to you to pay off your good debts even though you could make more money by putting your extra cash towards something else.

Summing up

I hate wasting time and money. And I bet you do too. Especially when it comes to paying off debt.

There's no good reason to miss out on precious months where you could have been enjoying freedom from your debts and the money saved by reaching that point. So be sure to choose the right method for paying off your debt: the Power Pay Off Plan.

Obviously not everyone is going to save as much as Sam did by choosing that method, but it'll almost always save you money compared to using the Snowball Method.

And there's no research I'm aware of that proves any advantage to using the Snowball Method. Sure, people have theorized that it might make you more likely to follow through due to the small wins that you get by paying off a bunch of little debts more quickly, but there's nothing compelling out there that *proves* it.

And besides that, there's nothing stopping you from enjoying small wins with the Power Pay Off Plan.

In most cases, the best choice is to be logical about this: go with the math; leave inferior, unproven, and more costly theories out of it; and enjoy the savings you'll get.

And if despite this knowledge you still want to give the Snowball Method a try, only do so if you've taken the time to figure out how much extra time and money it'll cost you, and have decided that the benefits from doing so are worth it for your particular situation.

Coming up

Now that you know how to pay off your debts while avoiding the pitfalls of blindly choosing popular one-size-fits-all solutions, it's time to learn how to maximize your odds of success. In the next chapter, you'll find out the secrets to doing just that.

The Secrets to Successfully Get Rid of Debt

> *"Attitude is a little thing that makes a big difference."* Winston Churchill

The small details that most people overlook are often the deciding factor in whether or not you'll be successful with your goals to get rid of unwanted debts.

So what's the big secret to success?

You've got to lay out your goals in a very specific way and have the right mindset.

I know that sounds overly simplistic at first glance, but stick with me.

Cultivating the right mindset is crucial

None of this will work if you don't have the right mindset.

First, don't fall for the whole "money is the root of all evil" thing.

Some people feel guilty at the thought of having lots of money. They've been taught that only selfish, greedy people are well-off — and since they don't want to be that kind of person, they self-sabotage by making bad decisions about managing their finances.

But having money isn't necessarily bad or good — it's how we use it that makes it one or the other.

For example, if right now you're deep in debt, you probably can't afford to donate to charities that are important to you.

But imagine how different it would be if you were firmly on the road to financial freedom, out of debt, and had money to spare — you could do so much good with that money now that you finally have enough of it. You could donate to causes that you believe in, help deserving family and friends, and so much more.

Additionally, if you take care of yourself financially, your loved ones won't have to stress out worrying about how you'll afford to take care of yourself. And you won't have to worry about it either.

The key takeaway is that having money is good if you put it to good use.

Second, understand that even if you stink at managing your debts right now, you can change.

Research proves that we are capable of changing ourselves. So even if you've always thought of yourself as being prone to getting into too much debt, this doesn't mean you're destined to always be that way.

"Believe you can and you're halfway there." Theodore Roosevelt

For example, you can adopt a growth mindset. "This growth mindset is based on the belief that your basic qualities are things you can cultivate through your efforts. Although people may differ in every which way — in their initial talents and aptitudes, interests, or temperaments — everyone can change and grow through application and experience." (Carol Dweck, Stanford University[4])

Third, go into this for the long haul.

It's very important that you go into this with the expectation that it'll take time to get rid of your debts. The last thing you want to do is feel down because "it's taking too long". It's normal for it to take significant time to get rid of debts, so don't beat yourself up over this reality, okay?

Also, if bad spending habits are what got you into debt, remember that it's normal for it to take time to change them.

According to a 2009 study published the European Journal of Social Psychology[5], it can take anywhere from 18 to 254 days for a new behavior to become a habit.

Don't let the "up to 254 days" depress you though.

I know that's a long time to wait for new attitudes and behaviors surrounding money to become habit, but, as the saying goes, "better late than never". And remember that some people were able to change their habits in as little as 18 days — maybe you'll be one of them!

In any case, a key takeaway is that you can create new and better habits as long as you persist and give it enough time to become automatic.

So whatever you do, don't quit too soon. And no matter how many days it takes your new ways of handling money to become natural, it's not as though it'll be all bad in the meantime — you'll still be making a lot of good decisions on your way there. And if you mess up, just dust yourself off and assess the damage, then come up with a plan to keep going in the right direction. Don't quit.

Now it's goal time

Once you know about the eye-opening research that's been done on goal setting, you'll be able to use this knowledge to dramatically improve your success rate with reaching your objectives for debt reduction and ALL other areas of your life.

Here are the small but powerful changes you need to make to maximize your odds of success.

S.M.A.R.T. Goals

If you want to set goals that you're actually going to accomplish, they need to be SMART, and have the following five characteristics.

1. Specific

Your goal should be easily understandable, not too broad, and have enough detail to make clear exactly what you mean.

Bad: Pay off debts.
Good: Pay off the $3642 owing on my Sears credit card within the next 2 months.

2. Measurable

Your goal needs to be measurable, so it's completely obvious whether or not you've reached it.

Bad: Save money.
Good: Put aside $500 in my savings account in the next 3 months.

3. Actionable

Ensure that your goal includes an action that you can take to attain it.

Bad: Save money on groceries.
Good: Cook rice as a side dish three times a week instead of using potatoes (which cost more per serving).

4. Realistic

Your goal needs to be something you have the skills, knowledge, and ability to actually do.

Bad: Win the lottery.
Good: Increase income by applying for two part-time job openings every day until I land one of them.

5. Time-bound

Whenever possible, include a deadline in your goals. This helps to prevent your goal from slipping away into the indefinite future.

Bad: Pay off my mortgage.
Good: Pay off my mortgage within 5 years.

But while ensuring your goals meet as many of the above criteria as possible is an excellent start, it still isn't enough if you want to completely maximize the odds of success. To find out how to do that, keep reading.

The 3-step secret recipe for success with S.M.A.R.T. goals

Okay, so this may not be a secret by the strictest of definitions, but since most people don't use this recipe for success, it might as well be a secret.

According to research[6], people who follow the recipe I'm about to share with you have a much higher chance of attaining their goals compared to people who don't.

And there are three major components of this recipe which we haven't covered in our previous discussion of SMART goals.

First, after you've written down your goals, jot down an "action commitment" for each one.

For example, if your SMART goal is to "Increase income by applying for two part-time job openings every day until I land one of them," your action commitment could be "Spend 1 hour per day finding job openings in my local newspaper and Craigslist that I can apply for."

Here's another example. If your goal is, "Pay off the $3642 owing on my Sears credit card within the next 2 months," your action commitment might be, "Sell my car to get the money required to pay off Sears credit card (and use public transportation instead of driving my own vehicle)."

And here's one more example for you. If your goal is "Put aside $500 in my savings account in the next 3 months," your action commitment could be "Stop spending $6 per day on a large Frappuccino at Starbucks for 84 days, and put that money into my savings account instead." (84 days x $6 per day saved = $504 cash saved up)

The second thing you need to do is share this goal and commitment with a friend.

And the last thing you need to do for this "secret" recipe for goal success is send a weekly progress report to your friend. This will hold you accountable.

The study compared goal setters who used some, or none of the above three techniques — the most successful were those who used all of them.

A big caution

Don't skip a single part of the above recipe for success. Because if you do, it'll probably make you less likely to achieve your goal. Here's why.

In an interesting study[7], researchers asked law students about their desire to make use of educational opportunities. Those who expressed a goal to make the best use of such opportunities were divided into two groups. One group had their desire to reach the goal of making best use of educational opportunities noticed by an observer, and the other group was able to keep their goal to themselves.

It turns out that the group who shared their goal spent less time, on average, making use of educational opportunities that were subsequently presented to them. Researchers theorized that this may have been because sharing their intentions to make the most of these opportunities created a "social reality" of sorts. That is, sharing the goal made it seem a bit like it had already been reached, so they didn't try as hard to make the most of it.

The solution

So how do you get around this? You create goals that are SMART (specific, measurable, actionable, realistic, and time-bound), you share them with someone, and you build in accountability by sharing progress reports.

You'll notice that in that study, the "goal" wasn't very specific, it wasn't measurable, nor was it time-bound. The lack of those three important parts of a SMART goal could be why sharing the goal wasn't enough to help them increase the odds of success. Additionally, there was no accountability process baked into that study.

I suspect that those law students would have done better if they'd created a SMART goal along with an action commitment such as, "I will study law for four hours a day, six days a week for 12 consecutive weeks, in addition to going to all required law school classes during that time period", plus shared the goal with the experimenter, and submitted weekly progress reports.

So when you're creating SMART goals for paying off your debts, ensure that all of your goals are specific, measurable, actionable, realistic, and time-bound. Don't forget your action commitment. Plus, when you share them with a friend, be sure to commit to regular progress reports that will put pressure on you to actually do what you set out to do in the first place.

One goal you must include on your list

One of the most important goals to include on your list is to stop borrowing more money. Because if you fail to stop, you're merely digging yourself into a deeper hole that'll be harder to climb out of.

Formulate a SMART goal in regards to stopping the borrowing cycle, and ensure that you use the above recipe for success to make it happen.

A note about credit cards

Here is an important point that you need to be aware of if you use credit cards.

If you have any credit card debt that you don't pay off in full each month, you should stop using your credit cards until you 100% pay them off, and come up with a plan to ensure that you'll never, ever, rack up credit card debt again.

Coming up

You've been armed with the knowledge you need to maximize your odds of doing what needs to be done to get rid of your debts. In the next chapter, you're going to get some ideas on how you can find the money to do it.

Where to Find the Money

"Change before you have to." Jack Welch

As discussed in an earlier chapter, one of the first things you need to do to become free of unwanted debts is get current on all of your payments.

And if you're not current on your payments, you need to figure out why that is. This is the first step to finding the money.

Getting organized

If it's merely because you're disorganized and forget to pay them on time (and not because you keep running out of money), getting current will be an easy task. All you need to do is set up a good reminder system, or automatic bill payments, and your issues will be mostly solved.

For a reminder system, try adding due dates for your monthly bills to an electronic calendar (for example, the one on your smart phone or computer), and set it to remind you ahead of time to pay it.

Or, you could make it a habit to pay your bills the same day you receive them, thus eliminating the possibility that you'll put the bill aside and forget about it.

For Mac and iPhone users

I've used the free calendar app on my Mac and iPhone to remind me to do all sorts of things, including paying my bills — it's a bit buggy, but for most people, it'll do the trick nicely — and you can set it to remind you up to five times before the due date. If you need something more sophisticated that can accommodate a lot more than just bill payment reminders, you can try the app I use now, which is Fantastical by Flexibits.

For PC and Android phone users

You can use the free Windows calendar app that comes with your PC, and use the Google calendar app for your Android phone. The two programs can be set up to sync with one another so that any data added to your phone calendar is automatically added to your PC version and vice versa.

There are tons of calendars to choose from, and if money is tight, there is almost certainly going to be a free one that will work for you.

For most people…

However, for most people, it's more complicated than that. Most people who don't make payments on time end up in that situation because they're running out of money.

There's obviously no magic bullet that I, or anyone, can offer you here.

But the good news is that if you put in enough work and have the right tools, the odds are high that you'll accomplish great things in regards to your debts. Even if you've never had any luck with it in the past.

"Opportunity is missed by most people because it is dressed in overalls and looks like work." Thomas Edison

So get ready to roll up your sleeves and find the money required to get rid of your unwanted debts.

Follow the money

The first thing you should do, if you haven't done so already, is start tracking every single penny that you earn, and every single penny that you spend. And keep this up at least until your debts are gone.

This is a simple, time-tested strategy that's extremely powerful and effective.

Here are four reasons why:

- It keeps you honest. Seeing where your money is going in black and white prevents you from lying to yourself about what you can afford.
- You'll find out whether or not you can squeeze more savings out of your existing earnings. Most people who go through this process find at least a few areas where they can easily cut back, and then put that cash towards paying off their debts faster.
- You'll know if you need to increase your income by getting a second job, or starting a home business.
- It makes it much easier to come up with SMART goals (specific, measurable, actionable, realistic, and time-bound) when you have concrete numbers to work with. Because you can't come up with specific AND realistic goals unless you're 100% sure of how much cash you can truly afford to put towards paying off your debt.

I go over the simple process I personally use to accomplish this in my book, *How to Stop Living Paycheck to Paycheck*. If you want an easy-to-follow, detailed explanation of how I track all this in only 15 minutes a week, plus the free tool I use to do it, be sure to check that out.

And if you already have your own system that's working well for you, then carry on using that.

If you need to bring in extra cash to pay off your debts

If you want or need to bring in some extra cash to pay off your debts faster, here are some ideas on how you can do it.

Cash in by selling things you don't need

You probably have stuff you don't need that other people will pay good money for — and that's what you're going to sell.

Look through your closet for classic clothing items in good shape that you don't need. If you have kids, gather up all the clothing they don't fit anymore that's not worn out. Arrange the clothing into attractive outfits, photograph it, and put a for sale ad up online.

If you have items that won't sell for much individually, combine into larger groups. For example:

> "Complete size 6 girl's wardrobe for $50.
> Includes 10 pairs of pants, 10 long-sleeve shirts, 6 pairs of shorts, 5 t-shirts, 5 tank tops, 1 formal dress, 4 sundresses, 3 skirts, 1 spring jacket, 1 raincoat, 1 pair of rubber boots, 1 snowsuit."

Or…

> "Gently used women's size 10 designer Giorgio Armani pant suit for only $95."

Do you have grown-up "toys" that you can part with? Maybe now is a good time to consider selling your expensive golf clubs that you only use a handful of times per year.

Perhaps your household can make do without a vehicle and use public transit instead — selling a car, SUV, van, or motorbike can raise some serious cash.

Or if you currently drive a really pricey vehicle, consider selling it and dividing the proceeds between buying a less expensive replacement and paying down some of your debts.

Start brainstorming ideas today for how you can raise significant cash by selling possessions you can do without. And don't forget that selling a bunch of low-value items can add up to a lot of money too — don't limit your brainstorming only to big ticket items.

Options for earning more money

1. Get a second job to work in addition to your current one.

2. Ask your employer if you can work more hours.

But if working another job (or more hours at your current one) isn't a good option for you, don't lose hope. There are lots of alternatives, and one of them is sure to suit you.

To begin with, why not consider working online? I know that may sound weird at first, but all kinds of people (even non-techies like me) have found great success with this in a wide variety of niches.

And that brings me to number three on this list.

3. I've personally been very pleased with a type of freelance ghost-writing I got into a few years ago that earns me as much as $60 per hour, despite starting out with no experience, no contacts, and no

credentials. I started out on a site called Upwork. If you want to find out more, I wrote about how I did it in my book, *Turn Your Computer Into a Money Machine*.

4. You could offer your services as a virtual assistant. Online business owners need help with all sorts of things, such as internet research, social media account management, email management, hotel and flight bookings, preparation of slide shows, and blog commenting, just to name a few possibilities.

Hop onto a freelancing website like (you guessed it!) Upwork and check out some of the job postings. There are tons of things that businesses are looking to outsource, and maybe you're the one they need.

5. If you're computer savvy, learn to set up WordPress websites and market your services to business owners and bloggers who don't want or are too busy to set it up themselves. I know a guy who was self-taught and eventually supported himself by doing just that. He landed his clients by networking with people in his local area.

6. Other people have had enormous success with network marketing. It's certainly not for everyone, but might be worth considering if you can find a product to market that you believe in.

7. Consider teaching conversational English online via Skype. And it doesn't have to cost anything to get started — it can be as simple as setting up a free profile on a freelancing site such as Upwork and applying for jobs until you land something. Another site worth considering is Fiverr — start out by offering a rate so low that it'll be impossible to pass up. Knock the socks off your clients with a top notch experience, and once you have some reviews start raising your rates for future clients.

8. Become a call center rep that works from home. Many companies don't have the budget for full-time call center staff, but could use some help. If you're home and able to take calls during their business hours,

this could be a good gig.

9. Browse Craigslist or your local newspaper for one-off odd jobs. You never know what might pop up.

Want more ideas?

When doing research for this, I came across an article in Forbes that suggested a website called FlexJobs.com. It's worth taking a look at their site to get ideas for the kinds of work you could do from home — there's a dizzying number of options, which is perfect for brainstorming purposes! While they charge a monthly membership fee to apply for jobs listed on their site, it's free to look around and get ideas.

You can do this

Whether you merely need to get more organized, or you flat out need an income overhaul, I'm betting on your success — because you can do this, my friend.

A little over two years ago I started a brand new career from scratch because I longed for a different kind of life than the one I was living. And this new career was entirely dependent on my ability to stare at a computer for hours each day, despite the fact that I was at one time incapable of looking at a screen for longer than 15 minutes — hell, I couldn't even keep my eyes open for an entire day without pain (I have crazy eye problems... it's a long story for some other time though.)

The point is, whether you're trying to earn extra cash for a complete career change as I did, or just to earn a few extra bucks on the side to help you pay off your debts, all things are possible.

And even if you don't see a solution right now, you need to keep your eyes wide open so that when one appears, you'll see the opportunity sitting in front of you and be able to act on it. Just because something is unworkable today (like working on the computer was for me at one time), doesn't mean it'll always be that way.

Stay strong. Stay optimistic. Believe in the potential for things to get better.

Action steps

If you need to earn more money…

1. Brainstorm ideas for ways to earn more money and make a list.
2. Choose an idea and take action — try it and see if it works. If it does, great. And if it doesn't, try the next item on your list.
3. Make full use of any opportunities you have, keep searching for better ones, and refuse to give up until you succeed at becoming free of unwanted debts.

If you have trouble keeping track of when your bills are due…

1. Brainstorm different methods of keeping track.
2. Choose the best idea and implement it. For example, try paying your bills as soon as you receive them, or get a calendar app and use it to remind yourself of any upcoming due dates.
3. If the idea works, stick with it. If it doesn't, keep trying alternatives until you find something that works for you.

Coming up

Now that you've got a plan for getting the money to pay off your debt, it's time to figure out how much cash you should be putting towards it in the first place. The next chapter will show you how to set yourself up for success, plus give you rules of thumb to follow and examples that illustrate how to apply them.

How Much Should You Pay Towards Your Debts

The simple answer is, "As much as you can!"

But since life isn't always simple, here are some factors to consider when deciding how much money you ought to put towards paying off your debts right now.

> *"Empty pockets never held anyone back. Only empty heads and empty hearts can do that."* Norman Vincent Peale

Set yourself up for success

To set yourself up for success, the first thing you need to do is ensure that you're making the minimum required payments on ALL of your debts. The last thing you want is to get behind on payments and ruin your credit score — not to mention the stress of having creditors hounding you.

After you've got that covered, I recommend that you make sure you have access to enough cash to cover any emergencies that may arise in future.

There are several schools of thought on how to handle this task.

The most conservative among us say the only acceptable option is to save up cash. Put it in a savings account and don't touch it unless, you guessed it, it's an emergency.

However, that's not always the most logical solution. Here are a few examples to demonstrate this.

Example 1

All the money Megan owes is credit card debt, and she's in the unfortunate position of having cards that charge outrageously high interest rates of 30%. Megan also has an <u>unused</u> line of credit at her bank that would only charge her 4% interest if she dips into it. Luckily, that line of credit also has a limit that's large enough to cover any emergency that might arise.

The first option is to put all of her extra cash into paying off those high interest credit card debts and not worry about putting aside cash for an emergency at this time. Because if the worst-case scenario happened, the line of credit can be used to cover it.

If her line of credit is large enough to use to pay off her credit cards, an even better option would be to do that and consider her credit cards to be her emergency fund until the line of credit is paid off (assuming she doesn't charge anything else to those cards!).

In this kind of situation, there's no logical reason for paying 30% interest on her credit card debt just so she can say she has cash saved up in her (presumably low-interest) savings account. The interest her savings account is paying won't cover the 30% that she's paying on her credit card balances, so there's no mathematical justification for putting cash there instead of towards destroying debt.

After Megan pays off her debt, then she can work on saving up some cash for an emergency fund.

Example 2

Ron owes $20,000 on a line of credit (LOC) charging 5% interest. He pays off his credit cards in full each month, so he owes nothing there. He's concerned about the fact that he doesn't have an emergency fund though, and has calculated that $10,000 in cash would be sufficient to cover any unexpected troubles. Another important piece of information is that if an emergency did come up, his credit cards would allow him to charge up to $30,000 on them.

Since the interest being charged on his debts is a sure thing and an emergency is not, plus, he has the means of paying for an emergency via credit cards in the unlikely event that one came up, Ron should prioritize paying off his line of credit. After that's done, he can start saving up for an emergency fund.

Of course, there are other scenarios where saving up a cash emergency fund should indeed be one of your first priorities. Here's an example of that kind of situation.

Example 3

Sara owes $15,000 on her car loan. That is her only debt. She does not have access to a line of credit or credit cards. The payment on her car loan is not flexible — the lender requires her to make a $500 payment every month, no matter what.

She currently has no emergency fund though, so if a big expense came up unexpectedly, she'd end up being unable to make her car payments and be at risk of losing her car and trashing her credit score.

She's debating whether or not to work on paying down her car loan faster, or save up for an emergency fund. She likes the idea of being debt free a lot though, and is in a hurry to get there as quickly as possible.

But in this case, since a large, unexpected expense would cause her to mess up her credit and potentially lose her car, she's better off saving up cash for an emergency fund. Once she has that saved up, she can start putting any extra money she has towards paying down her car loan sooner.

Rules of thumb for paying down debt

1. Always make sure you're meeting the minimum required payments.
2. Calculate how much money you require for an emergency fund.
3. Ensure that you can get your hands on enough cash to cover unforeseen emergencies via a savings account, credit cards or lines of credit.
4. Sort debts into good and bad debts.
5. Once you've established a source of emergency funds, put all extra cash towards paying off your bad debts.
6. If, at any time you use up your emergency fund, redirect all extra cash to building up the emergency fund again.

Here are more examples. For these scenarios, we're going to pretend your total minimum monthly payments on your debts are $2000 and you have an extra $500 per month that you've been putting towards paying off your bad debts faster (i.e. you're paying a total of $2500 per month towards your debts, but if you had to cut back, the bare minimum they'd allow you to pay is $2000 per month).

Example 1

You've calculated that you require access to 10k for emergencies and you have a 10k unused line of credit that is serving as your emergency fund.

A few weeks from now, an unexpected dental disaster occurred and you maxed out your 10k line of credit emergency fund to pay for it.

After this happens, you should go back to paying only $2000 per month (minimum payments) towards your debts, and redirect that extra $500 per month towards paying off your line of credit.

Once your line of credit is paid off (meaning your source of emergency funds is restored), return to putting the $500 per month towards bad debt repayment.

Example 2

You require access to 15k for emergencies and have 15k in emergency cash sitting in a high interest savings account.

A few months from now, you lose your job and end up using your emergency fund to keep afloat. A few months after that, you find a new job, but your emergency fund is down to only 3k.

At that point, you should go back to paying only $2000 per month (minimum payments) towards your debts, and redirect that extra $500 per month towards building up your cash emergency fund.

When you once again have 15k cash sitting in your emergency savings account, return to putting your extra $500 per month towards bad debt repayment.

Example 3

You estimate you require an emergency fund that gives you access to 10k. You have 5k cash in a savings account, and access to a 5k unused line of credit to cover you if a financial emergency comes up.

At some point in the future, due to illness, you end up having no income for several months. You max out the 5k line of credit, you use up all of the 5k in cash, plus you end up having to borrow 10k from your elderly parents.

Finally, you recover from your illness, get another job, and life goes back to normal.

Since this experience taught you that your emergency fund was at least 10k too small (because you had to beg your parents for a loan, and this created a financial hardship for them that you'd like to avoid repeating in the future), you should rebuild a bigger emergency fund this time. A good starting point is to aim for a new emergency fund that's 20k in size.

You should go back to paying only $2000 per month (minimum payments) towards your debts, and redirect that extra $500 per month towards paying back your parents, paying off the 5k emergency line of credit, and saving up 15k in cash.

Once the new 20k emergency fund access has been built (i.e. 5k line of credit is unused plus 15k cash in savings account), return to putting your extra $500 per month towards bad debt repayment.

Summing up

There's isn't one way to pay off debt that will be suitable for everyone. There are simply too many variables at play. Always take the time to do the math to figure out what makes the most sense for you. There are no shortcuts here. You've got to do the work. But I have complete faith in you and know you can do it. So get going!

The next chapter is going to give you a brief overview of things to consider regarding debt consolidation.

The Truth About Debt Consolidation

In theory, it seems like nothing about debt consolidation could possibly be bad. You consolidate your debts into one, get a lower overall interest rate that saves you money, and pay off your debts sooner.

But this is not always true and I'm about to explain why.

But before I get to that, there's another important trap you need to be aware of. Don't fall into the trap of allowing the good feelings you get from doing something about your debt (consolidating your loans) to lessen your drive to aggressively pay them off once and for all. Don't let those good feelings cause you to become complacent about your debt.

You can avoid that trap by creating S.M.A.R.T. goals that provide you with a clear roadmap for success, coming up with action commitments, sharing your goals with a friend, and making regular progress reports (as discussed in an earlier chapter).

Why debt consolidation may not be as good as it seems at first glance

While it may be obvious that you've simplified your life by combining multiple debts into one and getting a lower interest rate, it might not be obvious whether or not you'll save any money by doing so. And if you end up with an unscrupulous debt consolidation company, they may not tell you if their plan will cost you more in the long run. Because after all, the only way they make money is if they convince you to consolidate your loans with them.

Never forget that their interests may not be aligned with yours. It's on you to carefully think through any payment plans they suggest and make sure it's the best option before signing on the dotted line.

Here's an example to show you what I mean.

Example

Jan has the following loans:

- $10,000 at 15% interest that will be paid off in five years via monthly payments of $236. (Total of all payments = $14,160)
- $15,000 at 19% interest that will be paid off in five years via monthly payments of $383. (Total of all payments = $22,980)

Her total monthly payments will be $619 per month.

The debt consolidation company tells Jan they can cut her interest down to 14% and her monthly payments to only $429. At first glance, this sounds great — she gets a lower interest rate and lower monthly payments.

However, what they don't tell her is that she'll end up having to pay even more money over the long run.

If she stuck to her original two loans as they were, it would cost her a total of $37,140 to pay off the loans and they'd be gone within five years.

If she takes the debt consolidation company up on their offer, it'll take her eight years to pay it off (three extra years of making payments!) and cost her a total of $41,184 (i.e. $429/month x 12 months/year x 8 years).

The moral of the story is never take a consolidation company up on their offer until you've figured out how much it would cost you to pay off the loan using your current strategy instead. You might be doing fine as you are.

Protect yourself

Protect yourself from being tricked or taken advantage of by asking the following questions before agreeing to a consolidation plan.

1. Confirm the new interest rate, and how long it will be in effect for.

2. Confirm how long it will take before your debt will be paid off via their plan and the total cost of all those payments.

3. Ask your current lenders if there will be any fees incurred for moving your debt over to the consolidation company.

4. Ask the consolidation company if there are any fees for using their services and if so, how much.

Finally, make sure that all debt payments are being made throughout the process of investigating debt consolidation. The best way to do that is to make the payments yourself. Don't trust this important job to someone else.

Debt consolidation is NOT the same as debt

settlement

Debt consolidation is combining your loans from several lenders into one. Everyone still gets paid what they're owed. And as long as you continue to make all of the required payments on time throughout the process, and keep any previous commitments you've made, your credit score will be fine.

On the other hand, debt settlement companies can try to get you out of paying the full amount that you owe by, for example, negotiating with your creditor on your behalf. This is best avoided unless you literally have no other choice. Among other things, resorting to debt settlement can mess up your credit.

Summing up

If you're thinking of consolidating your debts, be sure to look out for the pitfalls you learned about in this chapter. Don't let anyone pressure you or rush you into making a decision. Take all the time you need to get a complete picture of how the process will work before deciding on a course of action. And remember that sometimes the old-fashioned way of leaving things alone and paying off your debts one-by-one is the best way to go.

In the next chapter, you're going to learn about insurance. That topic gets a bad rap, but it's crucial to know a few things about it and protect yourself from unexpected calamities that can trash your debt pay-off plans. You'll see which types of insurance I have, and get a list of other types to consider as well.

Insurance for the Unexpected

"To expect the unexpected shows a thoroughly modern intellect." Oscar Wilde

Prepare for the unexpected. This is one of the key tactics you need to have in your playbook if you want to maximize your odds of paying off, and staying out of, debt.

As you know all too well, there are no guarantees when it comes to finances. I'm a plan A, B, C, D, E kind of gal. I can never have too many backup plans for what I'd do if the financial crap hit the fan.

Sure, I've made plans for normal things like most people do.

But I can't help but take it a step further and think about what I'd do if the internet went offline forever (I currently earn my living online, so that would be a tad bit problematic), house prices fell by 50% (I invest in real estate, so this would be a HUGE disappointment), a massive medical problem left me unable to work for a prolonged period, and so on. How would I pay my bills? How would I ensure that I'm able to meet all the required payments on my debts?

And I'd like to encourage you to do the same for your own situation. The peace of mind you'll have after going through the process of creating solid plans to help you coast through any financial downturns is priceless.

Insurance is one of the key factors in how I plan for the unexpected. And it can help you too.

After looking at the various options for insurance that are available, and weighing the odds and costs of various calamities that can happen versus my ability to handle them on my own, these are the types of insurance that we've chosen to get and why.

Go through the list and see which ones might be beneficial for you to have as well. It will serve as a starting point that will give you some idea of the types of things you ought to be thinking about and discussing with an insurance specialist that you trust.

Term life insurance

When I was pregnant with our first son, we signed up for a 20-year term life insurance policy.

During the years that our kids would be too young to support themselves, we wanted to ensure that if either me or my spouse got creamed by a bus when crossing the street, fell off a cliff never to be seen again, or died from something more normal like cancer, the surviving spouse would receive the proceeds of a large enough life insurance policy to replace the income of the spouse that's gone until our kids were grown.

We figured once the kids are grown, the surviving spouse (whether it was me, or my husband), could fend for themselves alright. But if the unthinkable happened while our kids were still young, we didn't want to make it even worse by having to struggle financially.

Every year for the past nine years or so since starting our family we've dutifully paid that premium — even though it's substantial. Odds are we'll never make a claim on this policy (at least I certainly hope not!), but it's important for us to have it just in case.

Why term insurance and not permanent?

Because it was more affordable than the permanent varieties that pay out even if you die when you're old and grey. The higher premiums of the permanent policies didn't fit into our budget, and we knew we'll be able to make do without that kind of policy just fine.

Health insurance

If you already have adequate health insurance through your employer, or via government-sponsored care, feel free to skip this section. But if you don't, then read on.

It's crucial to get health insurance if at all possible. We've all heard of people for whom a medical emergency or serious illness royally screwed up their finances, caused a bankruptcy, or worse.

I don't know about you, but I'd like to do everything I can to avoid such a fate.

Tips for choosing the right health insurance plan

Ensure the maximum yearly coverage is high enough to cover even the most pricey illnesses. If you're unlucky enough to require brain surgery, get a form of cancer for which treatment costs hundreds of thousands of dollars, or run into some other nasty and expensive experience, the last thing you want to experience after the high of surviving wears off is to find yourself broke and owing a lot of money to the hospital.

Balance the coverage you're getting for your money against the cost of the premiums. For example, say for an extra $2500/year you can get a plan that covers all prescription medication, yet you generally only spend about $400 a year on medication. In a case like that, it may be worth your while to take a chance and scrap the prescription drug coverage to save money on your premiums. Assess your situation, discuss the pros and cons with someone in the know about medical expenses and risks (such as your doctor), and make the best decision you can.

Home insurance

An uninsured home is the equivalent of hiding money under your mattress. If the mattress caught fire, your money would be gone.

And if your uninsured home burns down, any money you put into it goes up in smoke. Literally.

So if you own a home, you have to insure it.

But when shopping around for insurance, be sure to look into exclusions on the policy too. For example, if your home is located on a flood plain, you may not be covered if a flood destroys your home. Knowing the exclusions means you have an opportunity to plan for the worst, increasing your odds of coming out of it on top.

Insurance to cover your possessions

Consider whether or not you can afford to replace your stuff if it were all stolen or lost in a fire. For this reason, we decided to play it safe and get the contents of our home insured too.

If you own your own home, this may be included in your home insurance policy. And if you rent, you can buy special insurance that's intended for renters.

Vehicle insurance

If you own a vehicle that you can't afford to replace with cash, make sure it's insured. In fact, in many jurisdictions, it's illegal to drive one at all if it's uninsured.

Liability insurance

Depending on where you live and how many assets you have, you should definitely look into this. For example, can you be sued in any of the following situations:

- someone slips on your sidewalk and gets hurt
- you're involved in a car accident which the other party thinks is all your fault
- you own rental property and your tenants think you made a mistake that's worth going to court over
- you make a mistake at work (medical professionals are one example of a group of people who generally require liability insurance to protect them in case they make a mistake at work)

So that's it for the types of insurance we have. But depending on your situation, there may be others that are worth considering.

Other types of insurance to consider

Disability insurance — look into this if you don't have a big enough nest egg to live off of in the event that you become disabled and unable to work.

Valuables insurance — your home or renters' insurance policy may already cover these, but if not, and you'd be devastated if they ever got lost or stolen, this could come in handy. This can be useful for collectibles, wedding and engagement rings, family heirlooms, and the like.

Umbrella insurance — this can help to cover a shortfall in coverage from your other policies. It can protect your assets from liability, bodily injury, and property damage claims, plus it can help cover any legal costs incurred.

Since I'm not an insurance professional, I highly recommend that you use the information here only as a starting point. Contact a licensed insurance broker in your area and find out if there are any other policies that they think you need. You may even want to compare the advice of multiple brokers. Consider what they say carefully and make the best decision you can.

Summing up

Now that you know how to pay off your debts and how to insure yourself against the unexpected, it's time to do a quick recap of the action steps you'll need to take to pull this off. After that, you get to the fun part, which is building wealth.

Action Steps Recap

There were several action steps spread throughout this book. Here is a recap all in one place.

1. Go through every credit card, every bank statement, every loan statement, every single bill you have, and find out how much debt you have.
2. Create a chart so the information is easy to read and well-organized. For every single one of your debts, write down the following information: what the debt is for; who you owe it to; the interest rate, the minimum monthly payment due, and balance owing; whether or not it's good or bad debt
3. Don't freak out.
4. Set up systems to automate bill payments as much as possible.
5. Figure out how much money you can afford to put towards your debts.
6. If you need to earn more money, brainstorm ideas, and take action to make it happen.
7. Investigate available insurance options and make sure you're adequately insured.
8. Make a list of SMART goals for getting rid of your unwanted debts right now. For each and every one of them, ensure that they are specific, measurable, actionable, realistic, and time-

bound. Include an action commitment.
9. Don't just memorize your list — you need to write it down somewhere that you can refer back to as needed. You can use a notebook and pen for this, or a document on your computer, laptop, or tablet.
10. Write down an action commitment for each goal.
11. Choose a trusted friend who is willing to hold you accountable. Share your goals and action commitments with this friend.
12. Send your friend weekly progress reports.

How to Build Wealth

"In reading the lives of great men, I found that the first victory they won was over themselves... self-discipline with all of them came first." Harry S. Truman

Once you get rid of your debts, you'll have all that cash that was going towards loan payments available to use for something else. And that presents you with a great opportunity — to use that money to create more money. This can help you to do a lot of good, not just for yourself, but for others too.

This is the beginning of your journey down the road to wealth and a secure financial future.

Now if you do a Google search for "how to build wealth", you may come across goofy ideas like coupon clipping. But last I checked, no one ever became wealthy from clipping coupons. Sure, it's great for saving a few bucks, but not enough to build significant wealth.

If you distill all the fluff out there down to only what actually works, you'll see that there are two main ways to build wealth. Each of these require an entire book to do them justice, but for what it's worth, here they are:

1. You can invest your money and build up a nice nest egg over time. There are lots of ways to do this — you can choose stocks, bonds, index funds. you name it. If you go that route, please get professional advice before putting any cash into it. As for me, I've chosen to invest in real estate.
2. You can plow that money into a great business idea. But be careful. Don't blow it all. Go slowly. Test as you go. Take baby steps. And don't go into more debt!

Sure, you can save your money in an account at your bank, but that's probably not going to increase your net worth after inflation is taken into account.

Take action

You read this book, and that's a good sign. But make sure you don't stop at reading. You've got to take action and implement the strategies you've learned in order to become free of debt.

You can do this — I believe in you. Don't give up. Keep going no matter what. And in the end, you'll be rewarded for your efforts.

Did You Enjoy This Book?

I want to thank you for purchasing and reading this book. I really hope you got a lot out of it!

Can I ask you for a quick favor though?

If you enjoyed this book, I would really appreciate it if you could leave me a review on Amazon.

I love getting feedback from my readers, and reviews on Amazon really do make a difference. I read all of my reviews and would love to hear your thoughts.

Thanks so much!

Avery Breyer.

More Books by Avery Breyer

How to Stop Living Paycheck to Paycheck

In this best-selling budgeting bible, you'll learn a complete system that takes only 15 minutes a week to maintain. You'll get the motivation and know-how to build up a big stash of emergency cash, details on how to find the money to get rid of debt, make sure you never run out of money, and avoid the 11 worst budget traps (that will ruin your financial plans if you let them!).

How to Raise Your Credit Score

Find out how to pump up your credit score and be approved for credit cards, loans, and mortgages with ease, plus, save money with the lowest interest rates that are only offered to the financial first class!

Turn Your Computer Into a Money Machine

Learn my tactics to earn as much as $60 per hour of my time, with nothing more than a computer and an internet connection - no prior experience required! I work WHENever and WHEREever I want, plus take time off whenever I please. Want to join me?

All books are available on Amazon in Paperback and Kindle formats.

Special Bonuses, Especially for You

As thanks for buying my book, I'd like to offer you **FREE access to 3 special bonuses I've prepared especially for you, that will help you on your journey.**

Here's what you get:

1. Instant access to my **Debt Destroyer Tool**
2. One day after that, you'll get access to my very informative **video interview with debt destroying dynamo Melanie Lockert**. This interview is **jam-packed with actionable tips** on handling the emotional highs and lows of dealing with debt, tips **for the average person** on how to get rid of it quicker, and so much more.
3. And a few days after that, you'll get access to an info-packed **interview with personal finance expert Michelle Schroeder-Gardner** — she has 2 undergrad degrees plus a **Finance MBA**, and **paid off her debts in only 7 months**. Listen to her interview and learn how to pull it off. She really knows her stuff!

Last, but not least, if I ever come across any other info that I think will be of use to you, I'll be sure to send it your way.

You're not alone in your journey to destroy your debt and feel the freedom that comes with that. Others have walked this path before you and are here to help. Ready?

Get Access Now!
https://averybreyer.com/your-road-to-wealth-starts-here-1/

Appendix

Housing Prices, Appreciation, and Inflation

In an earlier chapter, I told you that Michael shouldn't depend on appreciation as a source of making money over the long term on the lakefront cabin he was thinking of buying.

And I said the reason for that is that historically speaking, the rate of home price appreciation approximately matches the rate of inflation (if you take into account the increase in home sizes over the same time period).

Intuitively, you probably know this. Because if over the long haul home values increased at a rate that's faster than that of inflation, eventually no-one would be able to afford to buy a home. Or a lakefront cabin, for that matter.

But it can't hurt to prove it to ourselves by running the numbers.

First, there's a formula you need to familiarize yourself with:

Average % growth rate per year

$= [(C/P)^{1/Y} -1] \times 100$

C = current value
P = previous value
N = number of years

Next, there are three sets of data that we need to look at.

1. Median home price
2. Changes in home size (because increases in home prices over

the years are partly due to the fact that people are buying larger homes than they used to)
3. General inflation rate

We're going to assess the average % growth rate per year to confirm if our intuition about not being able to depend on long-term appreciation as a source of profit is accurate.

All numbers that follow are for new single family homes.

Median home prices

According to U.S. government census data[8], the median new home price in September 2016 was $313,500.

And according to that same data, the median new home price in September 1963 was $17,900.

Now, we'll calculate the average % increase in new home price over that 53 year period (i.e. 2016 - 1963 = 53 years) by using the formula above.

C = 313,500
P = 17,900
N = 53

If you plug those numbers into our formula as follows…

$[(313{,}500/17{,}900)^{1/53} - 1] \times 100$

… you get 5.6% for your average annual % increase.

Changes in home size

According to a United States Department of Commerce 1969 Construction Report[9], the median square footage of new homes sold in

1963 was 1365 square feet.

And according to the U.S. Census Bureau's Quarterly Starts and Completions report[10], the average of the median new home square footage for the first 2 quarters of 2016 is 2429 square feet.

Now, we'll calculate the average % increase in new home square footage over that 53-year period (i.e. 2016 - 1963 = 53 years) by using the same formula as above.

C = 2429
P = 1365
N = 53

If you plug those numbers into our formula as follows…

$[(2429/1365)^{1/53} -1] \times 100$

… you get 1.1% for your average annual % increase.

Average inflation

Finally, according to the BLS CPI inflation calculator[11], $1 in 1963 has the same buying power as $7.89 in 2016.

If we plug these numbers into our formula above, we end up with an average inflation rate of 4% as follows:

C = 7.89
P = 1
N = 53

$[(7.89/1)^{1/53} -1] \times 100 = 4\%$

Housing price increase due to appreciation

5.6% is the average annual increase in new home prices.

But if you consider that 1.1% of that increase is due to the increase in median new home size, and 4% is due to inflation, you're left with almost no appreciation (i.e. 5.6 - 1.1 - 4 = 0.5%)

Needless to say, 0.5% is such a pittance that it's really not worth considering. You can likely get a better return from sticking your money in a savings account.

And depending on which date range you choose your data from, the apparent return due to appreciation could be in the negative as well.

The point is, doing these calculations only provides us with a rough estimate. But any way you look at it, the rate of return from appreciation is not likely to be anything to get excited about.

The conclusion is…

Play it safe, and make conservative calculations when deciding whether or not a debt used to purchase real estate is good or bad, and don't take expected appreciation into account when determining if the debt is likely to turn a profit.

Look, we all know you could get lucky in a hot market and have real estate temporarily increase at a rate that's larger than the inflation rate.

But there is no guarantee that this will happen. And it's risky to depend on that for a return.

And as we learned in the 2008 housing crisis, real estate values can also crash in the short term.

1. Knowledge does not protect against illusory truth.
Fazio, Lisa K.; Brashier, Nadia M.; Payne, B. Keith; Marsh, Elizabeth J.
Journal of Experimental Psychology: General, Vol 144(5), Oct 2015, 993-1002
2. https://www.census.gov/housing/census/publications/who-can-afford.pdf
3. Winning the Battle but Losing the War: The Psychology of Debt Management. Amar, M.; Ariely, D.; Ayal, S.; Cryder, C.; Rick, S. Journal of Marketing Research, Vol. XLVIII (Special Issue 2011), S38-S50
4. http://www.mindsetonline.com/whatisit/whatdoesthismeanforme/
5. How are habits formed: Modelling habit formation in the real world. Lally; van Jaarsveld; Potts and Wardle. European Journal of Social Psychology, Volume 40, Issue 6, pages 998–1009, October 2010 http://onlinelibrary.wiley.com/wol1/doi/10.1002/ejsp.674/abstract
6. http://www.dominican.edu/dominicannews/dominican-research-cited-in-forbes-article
7. When Intentions Go Public Does Social Reality Widen the Intention-Behavior Gap? Gollwitzer, P.; Sheeran, P.; Michalski, V.; Seifert, A. Psychological Science, Volume 20, Number 5, 612-618 (http://www.psych.nyu.edu/gollwitzer/09_Gollwitzer_Sheeran_Seifert_Michalski_When_Intentions_.pdf)
8. https://www.census.gov/construction/nrs/pdf/uspricemon.pdf
9. https://www.huduser.gov/portal//Publications/pdf/HUD-11675_v2.pdf
10. http://www.census.gov/construction/nrc/pdf/quarterly_starts_completions.pdf
11. http://data.bls.gov/cgi-bin/cpicalc.pl?cost1=1&year1=1963&year2=2016

Printed in Great Britain
by Amazon